ARTISTS AT A SHIFT IN TIME

Courage in an Age of Conflict and Change

OTHER BOOKS BY
CHRIST JOHN OTTO

An Army Arising:
Why Artists are on the Frontline of the Next Move of God

Body
Where You Belong
Red Book of Poetic Theology for Artists

Bezalel
Image of God
Yellow Book of Poetic Theology for Artists

Mary
Honor and Value
Blue Book of Poetic Theology for Artists

Drip

VERY GOD
An Artist Explores the Nicene Creed

Artists at a Shift in Time

COURAGE IN AN AGE OF
CONFLICT AND CHANGE

CHRIST JOHN OTTO

BELONGING HOUSE MEDIA

Artists at a Shift in Time: Courage in an Age of Conflict and Change.
by Christ John Otto, Manchester, New Hampshire, USA.
Copyright © 2024 Belonging House Media, LLC.

Unless otherwise noted, all scripture quotations are from the Revised Standard Version of the Bible—Second Catholic Edition (Ignatius Edition) Copyright © 2006 National Council of the Churches of Christ in the United States of America. Used by permission. All rights reserved worldwide.

Scripture quotations marked (NLT) are taken from the Holy Bible, New Living Translation, copyright ©1996, 2004, 2015 by Tyndale House Foundation. Used by permission of Tyndale House Publishers, a Division of Tyndale House Ministries, Carol Stream, Illinois 60188. All rights reserved.

Scripture quotations marked (The Jersualem Bible) are from The Jerusalem Bible © 1966 by Darton Longman & Todd Ltd and Doubleday and Company Ltd.

Portions of the Prayer Rhythm for Artists are adapted from *The Daily Office SSF,* copyright the European Province of the Society of St Francis 2010. Material used with permission.

ISBN: 979-8-9874099-1-6

Library of Congress Control Number: 2024902315

For Derek

Rest eternal grant to him, O Lord:
And let light perpetual shine upon him.

May his soul, and the souls of all the departed,
through the mercy of God, rest in peace.
Amen.

Acknowledgements

Pulitzer Prize winning portrait artist Aileen Ortlip Shea once said "If you see a turtle on a fence post, you know they did not get there by themselves."

Self-publishing books is a huge undertaking, and this is my thirteenth attempt. This one in particular took eighteen months, and a number of tragic events occurred in the process, all of which slowed it down and increased the cost of production.

I am especially grateful for our Belonging House community. You are often the springboard and testing ground for my thoughts and ideas. I am blessed to have a very committed group of men and women who pray for me. Thank you Jim, Herman, Elizabeth, Rachel, Val, Zuzana, and Laché and those who receive my regular prayer updates. And of course, you cats keep me honest.

Thank you to everyone who gives at the fifty dollar or higher level on Patreon and Buymeacoffee: Barbara Anne, Tim, Jerry and Elizabeth, Martin, Karen, Heather, Derrick, Joe and Tammy, Vera, Deborah, Luann, Courtney, Betsy, Sean and Kirby, Lynski, Andrea, Steve, Brontis, Valencia, and Eric. Many of you have supported me for many years and not just your support but your friendship is a treasure. It is all about relationship.

Thank you to everyone who read the draft chapters under many titles on Substack. I am especially grateful for the feedback from Jörn Lange, Glenda Gibson, and Bill Wade.

Special thanks to Liz and Andy Dorton who have been a big part of the past year. Your friendship and help kept this project going. Thanks to Chris Mitchell for your friendship in this season.

Thank you to Benjamin Chua who made the editing process not only smooth but fun.

And of course, thanks Pete for all the proofreading over more than a decade.

TABLE OF CONTENTS

The Road in the Wilderness	1

Part I: The Artisans

Not About You	15
A Bigger Vision	21
The Goal	27
Global War	35
The Solution	43
The Charashim	51
Silence and Solitude	61
Magic	69
A Levite	79
Terror	85
A City Without Walls	95

Part II: David

The Generation of the Sons of Eli	103
The Point of No Return	117
Aligning Your Heart	123
Becoming a Warrior	131
Freedom from Trauma	139
Your Body is the Weapon	153
A Worship Revolution	163
The Throne of David	173

Part III: Daniel in Babylon

BY THE WATERS OF BABYLON	185
THE KINGDOM GRID	193
THE ANCIENT PATHWAYS	205
THE POWER OF GOING TO THE DANGEROUS PLACE	213
FOUR MEN IN A FURNACE	219
THREE TIMES A DAY	225
BABYLON IS DOOMED	233
A THRONE IN THE EARTH	241

Part IV: A Way Forward

THE END OF THE PILGRIMAGE	247
THE ANCIENT PATHWAYS:	
A PRAYER RHYTHM FOR ARTISTS	251
PRAYER IN THE MORNING	259
PRAYER THROUGHOUT THE DAY	265
NIGHT PRAYER	267
THE FIRE TEAM	275
HELPFUL PRAYERS	277
WORKS CITED	281
ENDNOTES	283

The Road in the Wilderness

Leonardo da Vinci was ahead of his time.
So was Vincent Van Gogh.
And so was Pablo Picasso.
And so is Ricky Raccoon,
and about a thousand
other people I found
when I did a quick search online for the words
"Ahead of his time."

**For hundreds of years,
artists have been described as
being "ahead of their time."**

Usually this cliché
is applied after the artist has died,
and after
they were misunderstood
by the conventional thinkers around them.
And as we all well know,
after their death,
the works they produced
sell for millions of dollars.
Lesser men
and weaker minds
benefit
from the ones who appear to be ahead of their time.

Picasso once said
that every act of creation is first an act of destruction.
He was talking about his mission as a "modernist"
to tear down the culture he inherited
and release his particular vision on the world.
Thinker Paul Kingsnorth
describes this process as the "great uprooting."[1]

It seems that the job of an artist
in the past one hundred years or so
was not the building
and establishing of something,
but rather,
**the destroying
of everything that came before.**

The best way for us to understand this
person who is ahead of their time
is to go on a journey into the wilderness.

There are trees,
mountains,
rocks and rivers,
and unknown things we are going to discover.

**History and culture
are like a road being cut through the wilderness.**
Most of the people walking
on this road find it to be well worn and smooth.
And most of them look for the easiest way to walk.
We call this the "path of least resistance."
And in school, and in society,
most people learn to take this path,
and to avoid taking risks
or upsetting the way things are.

This easy place is "how the world works."
These are established systems,
and by the time the majority of people—
the conventional thinkers—
come to that place in the road,

the system is well established,
and often
there are well known short cuts
that everyone has begun to take,
and those short cuts become
what we know as
corruption
in the system.

Many conventional people mistakenly think
that these roads just happen,
and ignore the price,
the risk-taking,
and the personal sacrifices brave individuals make
to establish a civilization.

Because of this mistaken view,
the vast majority of the people
on the path
have been taught
that to go off the path
is too dangerous to try.
"Stay in line."
"Keep your head down."
"Get a real job."
"Don't make waves."
"Go along to get along."
This is the way to a reasonably successful life.

And of course,
the worst thing a person can do is go off the path—
because there might be dragons in the woods.

**At the front of this pack of people
in the woods
is a small band
of courageous souls.**

These are the ones who, at
the same moment as the mass of people
are walking far behind them,

are surveying the terrain
and paying attention to the situation.

These folks are following
a narrow pathway
in the woods.
They are looking for ways to cross rivers,
and ways to get over rocks.
They have come upon grizzly bears and rattlesnakes,
and they are coming up with solutions.

These are the creative men and women who understand
that the world is a sea of problems,
and they have to first identify the problem
and then create a solution.

Although the mass of followers see them ahead,
they have no interest or understanding
in what they are doing.

In fact,
the great pack of people
are yelling to those up ahead.

"Hey you, get back in line!"
"Who do you think you are?"
"You think you can leave the pack and run ahead!"
"What you are doing is really irresponsible
and making us all look bad."
Now let's think about time again.
These two groups of people are on the same road,
and they see one another.
Look at your watch.
Notice,
they are living at the same time.
That group of artists and creative people is not
running ahead of their time;
they are running ahead of the pack.

They are living at the same time as the conventional crowd.
They are accurately seeing the problems and issues

of the times they are living in,
and they know that there is danger all around.
They know there are cliffs ahead that the whole crowd will fall off.
They know there is a rotten log that
someone once used to cross a river,
but that the mass of followers
behind them
is heavy and slow.
Those folks
will need
a bridge.

They know that the workarounds in the system
are now so corrupt that they are no longer helpful.

These folks are accurately understanding the times they live in.

They are, as the Bible describes,
like the sons of Issachar,
who rightly understood the times they lived in.[2]
The sons of Issachar were not prophetic;
they were observant.
These folks are not ahead of the time,
but are rather living keenly aware of the moment.
And most of the people in the pack are
either not thinking for themselves,
trying to get by day to day,
or simply are not interested.

Because the pack dwellers are the majority
they create the illusion that they represent the times.
They do not.

The pack is behind the times.
They are using roads someone else built,
and systems someone else created.
They are behind the times, not in them.

This perspective is the largest audience,
and so, mass media,
mass marketing,

and mass communication
puts the focus on them.
And this reinforces the perspective
that these are the times we live in.

It is an illusion.

Now look at this from another point of view.
Let's take an aerial view of the situation.

Deep in the woods,
way ahead of the group of creative people
is another group.
Some of them are alone,
and some of them run in little groups.
They are listening to God for themselves.
And God is leading them into deep and dangerous places.
These are the scouts and the pioneers.
These are the prophets and the apostles.
These are the ones
who are cutting a little path through the brush,
so someone can follow.
And as they walk into the unknown,
they discover an ancient pathway,
and learn that there is One who has been here before,
and that the ancient pathways never get old.

To the creative men and women
these forerunners are interesting and intriguing.
But to the pack of conventional thinkers,
they are wild-eyed crazies.
These are the ones who,
if you listen to them
will destroy everything you have come to know.
The creative people know
that the little path they found,
and the makeshift solutions along the way
were left for them
by the prophets and apostles.
**The forerunners give direction
and show the way for everyone else to follow.**

And then there is a fourth group.
This group drags at the end of the conventional pack.
And they tend to lag behind, and some sit by the way.
They are carrying heavy baggage filled with old stuff.
To us it looks like a lot of junk.
Big heavy books.
Beat-up furniture,
broken dishes,
and old clothes.

This is the church.
And it wasn't always this way.
Once upon a time,
it was the church that blazed a trail,
and led the way,
but a lot of bad thinking has taken over,
and the church,
with a few notable exceptions,
consistently lags about thirty years behind the center of culture.
And when the road begins to look scary,
instead of listening to God,
the church
sits by the road,
digs through their heavy baggage,
pulls out one of their old books
full of
what to think,
not how to think—
unquestioned answers to questions no one is asking—
and
begins to argue.

And some sit down
and never catch up.
And others die in the wilderness.

And when someone catches one of the adventurers
far ahead in the woods,
the church leads the call to have them punished,
and joins the side of those trying to stop the Kingdom.
They rip them apart on the internet,
have their books censored,

and call for their public humiliation.
They spread fabricated stories of scandal,
and stone the ones who can show the way.
And so, throughout history,
the religious folks kill the prophets
and stop the revivals.
And the culture cheers,
because now they can stay the same
on the broad road that leads to destruction.

In 2006,
an angel appeared to me
in my living room
and said:
"Jesus is calling you to raise up an army of artists
who will build him a throne in the earth."

I didn't know it at the time,
but God was calling me out of the pack,
and out onto the ancient, dangerous pathway.

About three years later, a wave of others
appeared on the scene
and they also began raising up artists.
One even used my ideas without asking,
but I,
like Paul,
accepted that the message I was called to carry
was spreading, even under someone else's name.

In 2013,
I published my book *An Army Arising*.
I was writing into a void
that I could see as others began to emerge.
I noticed that none of the "ministries"
appearing on the scene
understood the times we lived in,
and that God wanted to raise up artists
for a strategic purpose.
None of them understood the need for artists
to be deep disciples,

and none of them were helping artists
grow strong against the tide of culture.

In the Kingdom,
the WHY is always more important than the WHAT.
And the HOW is always the most important of all.

We are not living in ordinary times.

In 2005, God called me to a life of radical faith,
and I now know that this lifestyle is a prophetic act
in the face of gross commercialization.
My warnings to other leaders in private have gone unheeded,
and the majority of arts ministries
quickly moved to a sales and marketing model of ministry.

Instead of preparing artists
to lead in the times we live in,
times of conflict and war,
these ministries
catered to the American church
and tried to make as much money as possible
in the shortest amount of time
from conventional marketing methods.
They all had short-term successes of three to six years.

In most of the evangelical church world,
successful marketing is considered credibility,
and many know how to sell things,
but have no marketable product.

And a majority of the artists I meet,
seventeen years after I started,
still are not deep disciples of Jesus,
still quote Marx
and think it is the Sermon on the Mount,
and still act in a childish, precious, and immature way
about their art
rather than like professionals,
willing to learn their craft,
take risks,
and work hard.

I've now seen two waves of arts ministries come and go,
and have now noticed a third one beginning to emerge,
with all the same underpinnings of the previous two.
So far, it seems
no one is learning from this cycle
and the gap that I began writing into in 2012
still exists.
The idea of raising up an army
implies a time of war.
Until recently,
it was a cold war.
It was a war of ideas
and visions of both the past and the future.
It was happening
thirty years ago
when I was a student.
I was completely blindsided
when my ordination process became a battle in this war,
and no one prepared me for
the lies,
accusations,
stalling of my career,
and financial ruin that would follow.

I learned the hard way
that one behaves differently
in a time of war than in a time of peace.
Those folks in the pack
and lagging behind
do not understand the nature of the war
or the nature of their enemy.

It is a war of worldviews
and a war over who controls
how stories are told.
It is a war over what words are allowed to be used,
and, increasingly,
who is and who is not
allowed to tell stories.

It is a war against all that is true, good and beautiful,

and the belligerents are determined to win.
When I began this book,
the war was still simmering,
and in the midst of the writing,
the war got hot.
I have been shocked
at how things I wrote in 2022
and early 2023
have become eerily prophetic.

This is a strategic book,
and I believe the
calling on the artist
for this moment,
in the midst of a five hundred year shift
and in the midst of war,
is far more important
than I understood in 2012.
We are in the midst of the greatest shift
yet to be faced in human history,
and it is leading us to the return of Jesus Christ.

This book is arranged
in four sections.
The first is a deeper study into the vision of Zechariah
depicting a global war of ideas, and God's solution:
an army of artisans.

The second part is
going to be harder to grasp.
We have to look at a shift in time,
much like the one we are experiencing now.
We are going to look at the end of one age
with the Sons of Eli,
and the birth of another one under David.
We are going to look at David,
the trouble he endured
and how being an artist is part of the larger calling to be a warrior.

Like a musical symphony,
I introduce some complicated ideas that require a slower read.

Most important is the promise God gave David
that one day the Messiah would sit on his throne,
and how this promise is for us,
artists and creative people.

Then we are going to look at the ways
Daniel and his friends
found a way to not only survive in the court of Babylon,
but to overcome and succeed.

And finally,
I end this book with the models of prayer and discipleship
that I use every day.
It is the practical process we use in our community
to build disciples.
We have worked this out together over years,
and we know it works.

This book is for you
who are called to cut that path in the wilderness
for others
so that we can prepare a way
for the coming of the Lord.

Part I

THE ARTISANS

Not About You

It's not about you.

Conventional wisdom says, don't start a book that way,
because the reader will stop reading.

Let me say it again.

It's not about you.

Really.
It is not
about
you.

In 2012, I set out to write a book that made
no apologies to Christians
about being an artist
and for art in general.

Today we have a different problem.
To counteract the way the church has treated artists,
many have taught that being an artist makes you special.
It's all about your expression,
your destiny,
your success.
I live in London,
and several times every day

a person
who is looking at her electronic device,
and often talking on speaker,
having a conversation
about deeply personal and private matters,
walks right in front of me
or right into me.
She does not look up,
and never apologizes.
                        These people make me miss my bus.

We live in a narcissistic age.

It is not about you.

For many years,
I worked in the charismatic church world,
and with many "prophetic" people.
Often these people are real trouble.
So many of them came around and tried to
sabotage our community that
I had to get counseling
and learn about
Narcissistic Personality Disorder.
I discovered the hard way
that the prophetic movement
and the prophetic arts movement
seems to attract
narcissists.

A narcissist is a
person who is the center of their own universe
and who is unable to empathize with
the needs and feelings of others.
Empathy is the key.
We all have selfish moments,
but a real narcissist doesn't comprehend that you can feel pain
because they are using you to get their needs met.

This is important for this book,
because God called me to raise up an army.

We are living in a global spiritual war,
and the church still thinks that it can be slow,
unstrategic,
and immature.

And if you are going to fully grasp
the role of the artist
at the end of time,
you have to understand the foundation.

If you are gifted and talented,
if you are anointed,
if you are highly creative,
or if you have a big call from God,
that does not necessarily mean you are special.

The Kingdom of God begins here:
Take up your cross and follow me.
What will it profit a person to gain the whole world
and lose their own soul?
Many who think they have found their life in this world
will lose it.
Many who lose their whole lives will find it.

This is the foundation of being a disciple.
The church has taught us that this level of commitment
is for the super-saint,
but the New Testament makes it clear
this is the baseline of discipleship.
Bonhoeffer said,
"When Christ calls a man
he bids him come and die."[3]

God wants to strategically use
artists
who
are disciples
of Jesus Christ.

And so,
before I talk about time

and the times we live in,
before I can talk about the artist
and how the definition of being an artist is changing,
before I can give you some practical guidance
on how to manage the tectonic shifts happening today,
we have to talk about this reality:
It is not about you.

Are you motivated by financial success or a big platform?
Are you driven by book sales and marketing strategies?
Are you more concerned about your likes and followers on social
media than about the substance of your content online?
Do you spend more time trying to get attention
than you do in skill development
or in the secret place of prayer?

There are two questions
that great spiritual directors ask.
A monk once asked a newcomer these two questions
at the gate of the monastery.
What do you want, and what do you fear?

What do you want?
Really.
What do you want?

> And don't give me the good Christian answer,
> or the answer that you think is right.
> Some of you really just want to
> get rich,
> be famous,
> and live happily ever after.
> I'm not going to judge you,
> I just want you to be honest
> to you
> and to God.

Consumer Christianity has discovered
that you can use religion
to get rich quick.
Just look at the contemporary worship music industry,
or the big five American publishers
that now own all the Bible publishers.

Don't rush past this question,
because what you really want is what drives you.
And that want will determine,
in the end,
your methods,
models,
and motivations.

And the second question is equally clarifying.
What do you fear?

Think about that one.
My biggest fear is rejection.
Over the years, I have made more than one bad decision
trying to avoid rejection.
You need to be honest
with you
and with God here too.

I ask these questions right up front,
because this is not your typical book for Christian artists.
We are living in unprecedented times,
where technology and culture
are moving faster
than most people even understand.
We are talking about substance in this book,
not about methods
and trends.
**We are talking about your center as a human being
and as an artist.**

And in order to do that,
you have to understand
what motivates you
and what you really value.
And do those values and motivations
agree with the
Kingdom of God
presented to us in the New Testament?

Who are you living for?
Are you the center of your universe with a religious veneer,

or is God the center?
What do you want
and what do you fear?

We are living in big times,
and what God is doing in these times is bigger
than people painting in the corner of the church,
selling stuff online,
selling their courses,
and building a platform.
The destiny of planet Earth
is at stake.

It is not about you.

A Bigger Vision

Many of the artists and creative people who come to me
continue to struggle with shame and confusion over being an artist,
and whether or not being an artist is even valid.
When I wrote *An Army Arising*,
I had one goal:

> **To write a book for Christian artists
> that did not begin with an apology,
> or an attempt to reconcile
> evangelical theology with the arts.**

That simple goal opened the proverbial "can of worms."
I had to go places that other writers before me could not go.
Rookmaaker and Schaeffer were great thinkers,
but they were unwilling, or unable to question,
the principles of the evangelical grid.

Curiosity led me down a path of discovery
that has forced me to rethink
even my core understanding
of the Christian faith.

I have written many books about what I have learned:

That the words in Greek and Hebrew
for artisan, icon, and imagination
have been intentionally mistranslated or obscured.
That the second statement in the Decalogue
was split to form two commandments,

in order to expressly forbid making images.[4]
That John Calvin left the last eight chapters of Exodus
out of his commentaries,
to end the book with the golden calf,
resulting in the suppression of Bezalel in commentaries and teaching.

That the building of Saint Peter's Basilica
was directly funded through the sale of indulgences,
and that some of that money was
redirected to pay Michelangelo and Raphael,
and also funded a homosexual harem at the Vatican.
This causal link between the Reformation and the arts
stays with us to the present.[5]

And because I have not tried to hide the things I discover,
I have had a hard time finding
agents,
publishers,
or even reviewers
for my work.

I was offered a place to do my Ph.D.
at the Institute for Theology, Imagination
and the Arts at St. Andrew's.
I turned it down simply because the future of the academy
is murky, and I wasn't sure the academy was the best place to put my energy,
even for the credibility it might give me with people
outside my audience.

I am very grateful for our Belonging House community,
who understands what I am doing,
and who grasps that to truly
raise up an army of artists
we have to build on a real foundation.
That little goal,
to not apologize for art and artists,
has kept me busy for over ten years.

The goal was achieved,
largely because of a word that appeared in Zechariah 1:20.
The word was "charashim."

It appeared in my Morning Prayer readings,
and became the foundation of a long word study.
That word is translated
"craftsmen,"
"carpenters,"
or "blacksmiths" in most English Bibles.
Its original use,
found in Exodus 35:35,
**refers to a master artisan
overseeing all the arts.**
Charashim is used thirty-five times in the Old Testament,
always with this point of reference.

**My study led me to rethink what the Bible says about artists;
it propelled me to write two books on Bezalel—
the first in the English language—
and rethink everything I am doing
when I disciple and train creative people.**

I have now spent over ten years meditating on Zechariah 1:14-2:5.
Over the next few chapters I want to unpack this passage
and help you get a bigger picture of what God is saying and doing.
God's vision for the arts is much bigger
than selling stuff,
painting in the corners of churches,
making our church services more creative to draw bigger crowds,
or even fulfilling your destiny.

I want to impart to you a bigger vision.

So before we go there,
let's talk about the context of that passage in Zechariah.
In this book I am not going to make apologies for
solid Biblical study.
Too often we give artists "a pass" and dumb down things
to keep them in our churches, so that we can get them to do things.
Artists are smart people,
so I think you can handle it.

A bad habit that developed during the Reformation
is how you do theology.

**We have been taught to begin with an argument
and then find scripture verses
that support our conclusion.**[6]
This practice arose out of the academy.
Today, academic papers
and major denominational decisions are still made this way.
I have seen this method used to support
abstaining from alcohol,
forbidding the arts,
creating megachurches,
banning women from leadership,
ordaining women,
and allowing same-sex marriage.

Jesus told us to judge a tree by its fruit.
When you look at the church and the culture,
what you see is chaos reigning in every direction.
This model is a crazy way to discover the truth.
As Saint Paul told us,
"our God is not a god of confusion but of Shalom."[7]

Because of this approach to the Bible
most people that I talk to and teach
miss what the Bible is really saying.
When we read scripture,
we immediately either try to grab a "money quote"
to prove our point,
or immediately jump to interpretation.
The Bible is not designed to be read this way.
Context is everything.[8]

When we read Biblical prophecy,
three things might be happening.

There is the meaning for the **original** hearer,
then there is the **future** possible fulfillment
(not all Biblical prophecy is about the future),
and finally,
there are the implications for all times and places,
the **universal message**.
Often a passage will have all three layers.

The book of Zechariah was created
at the end of the seventy year exile of Israel in Babylon.
It begins with God showing Zechariah
angels who have surveyed the world,
and the world is at rest.
This is a time of peace.

And then Zechariah asks a question.
"Lord,
if the world is at peace,
what about Israel who is in exile
and Jerusalem that lies in ruins?
Will you have no mercy?"

This is how we develop in our relationship with God.
We need to always come to God and have a conversation.
The Lord is not afraid of our honesty.

And the Lord answers Zechariah
in a gracious and comforting way.
God sends an angel to speak with Zechariah
to give him a heavenly perspective.

"So the angel who talked with me said to me,
'Cry out, Thus says the Lord of hosts:
I am exceedingly jealous for Jerusalem and for Zion.
And I am very angry with the nations that are at ease;
for while I was angry but a little they furthered the disaster.
Therefore, thus says the Lord,
I have returned to Jerusalem with compassion;
my house shall be built in it,
says the Lord of hosts,
and the measuring line shall be stretched out over Jerusalem.'"[9]

Zechariah is asking,
"God, don't you care
and don't you see?
The whole world is prospering and we are still suffering."

And God says,
"Not only do I care and see,
I am moved by what I see.
I am going to look at Jerusalem with compassion,

and I am going to restore the temple
and the city."

**God sees the problem,
and when God sees a problem,
he brings a solution.**

This is the context for the beginning of Zechariah.
And as I said earlier,
to the original hearer,
this was about the end of exile,
and the restoration of Jerusalem.
We want to also read this from a
New Covenant,
Kingdom perspective.
This will make more sense when we read the rest of the chapter.
All those who are in the New Covenant
are Jerusalem and Israel.
In the New Covenant,
believers in Jesus the Messiah
are temples of the Holy Spirit.

God sees the problem,
and always provides the solution.
God's goal in Zechariah
is prosperity.

The Goal

God is in the details.

When you sit with the Bible,
you discover that there is always more.
The God of the Bible is the same God
who made the universe,
made atoms,
and sub-atomic particles,
and all the bio-diversity of planet Earth.
Honestly,
the problem with most people
is the size of their God.
The God of the Bible
is bigger
than everything human beings know.

There are some really interesting details
in this first chapter of Zechariah.

In Zechariah's encounter with the angel,
he communes with him.
In other words,
they spend time together
in fellowship with God.
And the angel tells Zechariah to proclaim.
Some versions of this say,
"Cry out,"
and others say, "declare."

**Part of the job of a prophet
is to listen to God on behalf of other people.
And another important part
is to speak out the things that God is saying.**

The word for calling is closely related to the word
for creation in the first chapter of Genesis.
God's word,
as it says in Isaiah 55,
will not return void.
And the prophet,
in speaking out the word of God,
not only proclaims the message,
but engages in making the message happen.

In our Belonging House community,
we bless the new moon at the beginning of the Jewish month.
We began doing this in 2012,
when our ministry was based in Salem, Massachusetts.
It was during a time when we were suffering continual
witchcraft attacks.
Blessing the moon dramatically shifted things.
In saying these ancient Jewish prayers,
I began to realize how powerful blessing is.
Not only has it manifested in the Jewish community through time,
but we have seen it manifest
in our community of artists and creative people.

The prayer begins like this:

May it be your will, Lord, God of our fathers, that you begin for us this month for good, and for blessing. May you give us long life, a life of peace, a life of goodness, a life of blessing, a life of sustenance, a life of physical health, a life in which there is no shame or humiliation, a life of wealth and honor, a life in which we love your Word, and fear God, a life in which the Lord fulfills the requests of our hearts for good. Amen.

This blessed life
is very similar to the life
described by Moses
in Deuteronomy:

And if you obey the voice of the Lord your God, being careful to do all his commandments which I command you this day, the Lord your God will set you high above all the nations of the earth. And all these blessings shall come upon you and overtake you, if you obey the voice of the Lord your God. Blessed shall you be in the city, and blessed shall you be in the field. Blessed shall be the fruit of your body, and the fruit of your ground, and the fruit of your beasts, the increase of your cattle, and the young of your flock. Blessed shall be your basket and your kneading-trough. Blessed shall you be when you come in, and blessed shall you be when you go out.

The Lord will cause your enemies who rise against you to be defeated before you; they shall come out against you one way, and flee before you seven ways. The Lord will command the blessing upon you in your barns, and in all that you undertake; and he will bless you in the land which the Lord your God gives you. The Lord will establish you as a people holy to himself, as he has sworn to you, if you keep the commandments of the Lord your God, and walk in his ways. And all the peoples of the earth shall see that you are called by the name of the Lord; and they shall be afraid of you. And the Lord will make you abound in prosperity, in the fruit of your body, and in the fruit of your cattle, and in the fruit of your ground, within the land which the Lord swore to your fathers to give you. The Lord will open to you his good treasury the heavens, to give the rain of your land in its season and to bless all the work of your hands; and you shall lend to many nations, but you shall not borrow. And the Lord will make you the head, and not the tail; and you shall tend upward only, and not downward; if you obey the commandments of the Lord your God, which I command you this day, being careful to do them, and if you do not turn aside from any of the words which I command you this day, to the right hand or to the left, to go after other gods to serve them.[10]

In his communion with the angel
Zechariah is commanded to make a proclamation.

He is to proclaim
that God's cities

shall spread and increase
in prosperity.
And in this prosperity,
the Lord shall prosper Zion
and bring comfort to Jerusalem.

**God's plan
is prosperity.**

When I was first learning to listen to the Lord,
the Lord showed me a property and told me to begin praying for it.
We began praying for this house,
and it became a big adventure.
I learned a lot about myself,
the nature of people,
and the real estate market.

One day, I was out prayer walking,
and the Lord showed me another property.
And the Lord said to me,
"I want that one too."
I was already involved with the big old house and that was not going very well.
In those days, I was still ministry minded,
and I thought we needed a property to build a ministry.
As my discussion with God became more heated,
the Lord,
in his loving, Fatherly way,
spoke to my soul.
"Son, you do not understand;
I want all of it. That's the goal."
And of course, I now know God wants people,
not property.

The Kingdom of God is always advancing.
As I said at the beginning of this book,
it's not about you or your ministry.
It's not about your destiny or career.
It's about a bigger thing.
God does want you to prosper,
but not just you.
He wants planet Earth to prosper,

and in prospering you,
he wants those around you to prosper—
even those who probably don't deserve it.

And prosperity is bigger than bank accounts.
Prosperity is shalom:
a whole relationship
with all of creation.
This is the vision that Paul refers to in Romans 8:21-22:
that all creation longs for the freedom
of the children of God.

God wants you to be blessed
so that you can be a blessing.
Again, it's not about you.

Zechariah 1:17
has no limits.
God's desire is that every city
spread abroad
would prosper.
And that prosperity
ultimately
would bring comfort and glory
to his Kingdom.

Every city on earth
is intended to look like the City of God.

I've spent most of my life in cities.
A lot of that time was spent in the inner city,
in Akron, Ohio,
Boston, Massachusetts,
and London, England.
I've seen drug deals,
and watched heroin addicts shoot up, right in plain sight.
The son of one of my prayer team members
was shot in the face
in front of a crowd of people
in Copley Square in Boston.
I have watched historic buildings
in London get covered with spray paint.

I have worked for years in racial reconciliation,
crossing racial and ethnic barriers,
only to be told I am a bigot with white privilege.
And I have watched government officials
continue to come up with
self-serving solutions to the problems they created.
No matter the party,
left or right, or nation or state,
the solutions always seem to be
"give us more money
and then we will be able to fix what we have broken."

**One thing I have seen in decades of inner city work
is the complete lack of
creativity
when it comes to solving problems.**

If there was a color of the inner city,
it would be the bleak gray of weathered concrete.

None of this is God's plan.
Like Zechariah,
I have cried out:
we will be blessed in the city
and blessed in the country.
Violence will no longer be heard in our land
nor blood in our borders.
Fathers will turn their hearts to the children
and children to their fathers.
The storehouse will be full.
We will be the lender and not the borrower.

God has a goal.
Actually, the goal that is stated in Zechariah 1
is fulfilled in the book of Revelation.

> And the city has no need of sun or moon to shine upon it, for the glory of God is its light, and its lamp is the Lamb. By its light shall the nations walk; and the kings of the earth shall bring their glory into it, and its gates shall never be shut by day—and there shall be no night there; they shall bring into it the glory and the honor of the nations. But nothing un-

clean shall enter it, nor any one who practices abomination or falsehood, but only those who are written in the Lamb's book of life.[11]

God's goal is a city
where nothing is hidden and all is full of light.

God's goal is a city,
where kings and leaders
bring the best of their nations and cultures for all to enjoy.

God's goal is a city
that is safe,
where the doors are open,
where there are no locks or barbed wire fences.

God's goal is for righteousness and sanctity,
a city without a red light district
or crime.

God's goal is a city without
graft,
corruption,
dishonest media,
or shady dealings.

God's goal is prosperity.

And that prosperity begins from the inside.
The little letter of Third John contains this precious blessing:
**May you prosper and be in health,
even as your soul prospers.**[12]

As with everything in the Kingdom of God,
the outward manifestation
of prosperity
comes from an inner manifestation in the heart.
This is why the city in Revelation
is full of those whose names are written
in the Lamb's book of life.
The only way prosperity can manifest
is through the transformation of the human heart.

Let's recap what we have learned so far:

Zechariah is grieved at the exile of Israel,
and cries out to God.
God sends him an angel
and tells him that He sees the situation,
and is moved with compassion.
And then God tells Zechariah
to proclaim
that God is going to spread his cities and prosper them:
and in doing this, bring comfort to Zion
and Jerusalem.

And then God tells Zechariah how.
It involves a global war.

Global War

The Bible often shows us the end
before the beginning.
**God does this
to instill in us
prophetic hope.**

How many centuries did the Jewish people
hold onto hope
that one day they would return to their homeland?
This concept is so strong
that the national anthem of Israel is HaTikvah:
"The Hope."

Christian believers too
hold onto hope.
We proclaim every Sunday:

Christ has died,
Christ is risen,
Christ will come again.

**Jesus Christ promised that he would return
and establish his Kingdom in fullness on earth.**
This hope has kept the saints going
for many centuries.
Zechariah was given the goal:
cities that spread abroad in prosperity.
That is the hope.

It's good news.

And then,
Zechariah looks up and sees a terrifying vision.
To us,
it seems like an odd picture,
but to Zechariah and the original hearers of this book,
it was a very clear picture.

We miss a lot in the Bible for two reasons:

We do not **understand the symbolic language**
that was universally understood
in the Ancient Near East,
and

We do not understand
the **significance of numbers in Hebrew thinking.**

A dear friend, the late Ethel Doolittle,
had a calendar with illustrations from the book of Zechariah
that she kept up all the time,
even though it was old and out of date.

In all honesty,
the pictures were a bit weird.
The visions that Zechariah saw were strange,
and without some serious deciphering,
to the modern reader are almost impossible to understand.

God gives Zechariah the goal:
prosperity.

And then Zechariah looks up.

> And I lifted my eyes and saw, and behold, four horns!
> And I said to the angel who talked with me,
> "What are these?"
> And he answered me,
> "These are the horns which have scattered Judah, Israel, and Jerusalem."
> And I said, "What are these coming to do?"

> He answered,
> "These are the horns which scattered Judah, so that no man raised his head . . ."[13]

So let's start unpacking this,
because it is really important for our study
on the artist at this shift in time.

The number four is a very important number in the Bible.
There are several places
where a prophet encounters four angels,
cherubim,
or creatures.
Probably the first place that comes to mind is
from Revelation chapter four,
where John sees four living creatures:
one like a lion,
one like an eagle,
one like an ox,
and one like a man.

Four always symbolizes the four cardinal directions:
north, south, east, and west.
Remember,
this is a world
where people were much more in tune with the earth
and their natural surroundings than we are.

This is a world
where no one had a compass,
a map,
or a global positioning system.
So the cardinal directions had to be sorted out
by looking at the stars.
And when one looks at the stars
in order to tell direction,
one starts to take in the vastness of the universe.
In the first chapter of Genesis,
on the fourth day,
God put lights in the sky to tell time and find direction.

**Four,
then,
became a symbol for the whole created order,
for the earth,
and for the universe.**

So whenever someone sees the number four in the Bible,
it is a symbol
for the world,
the universe,
and the entire created order:
all of creation.

The horn is also an important symbol in the Old Testament, especially in the Psalms. Here are just three of the many references to horns in the Psalms:

The Lord is my rock, and my fortress, and my deliverer, my God, my rock, in whom I take refuge, my shield, and the horn of my salvation, my stronghold. (Psalm 18:2)

All the horns of the wicked he will cut off, but the horns of the righteous shall be exalted. (Psalm 75:10)

But thou hast exalted my horn like that of the wild ox; thou hast poured over me fresh oil. (Psalm 92:10)

Imagine you are in a world
where there are no firearms,
or steel tools.
Imagine your best form of defense
is a sling and a stone.

Now imagine yourself with a herd of sheep,
and many of them have horns.
And then, of course,
there are the cattle,
who also have serious horns.

These horns are weapons.
You will get killed
if you are gored by a bull,

and you can get seriously injured
if you get in the way of an angry ram.

Across the ancient world
the horn became a symbol for raw power.
**It is the symbol of military might
and power over people.**

When David received the Kingdom,
it was his horn that was exalted.
His army won.

And the sound of a horn is also a rallying cry,
and the messenger of battle.
It is power and communication.

So we are seeing a symbolic vision that Zechariah
probably understood:
It is a
unified
global
army.
He is seeing global powers that have aligned with one another.
They are acting in unity,
much like the nations who gathered to build the Tower of Babel.
And this power is the power of communication.

And what are they doing?
These horns are putting out a message.
And the message is designed to do one thing:
scatter God's people
and bring them to the point of despair
so no one can lift up his head.

The horns declare one unified message
from the four corners of the earth
over and over again
until that message seems more real than reality.

**For the first time since Babel,
all the nations are in tandem
with one purpose:**

**destroy Israel,
destroy Jerusalem,
and make anyone who loves God
give up in despair and quit.**

Can you hear the heaviness in this?
Good is evil,
evil is good.
Only the strong survive.
Laws are for the little people,
and only the important and connected
receive a fair shake.

No one can look up.
The message is one of hopelessness.
Nothing is going to change,
and nothing is going to get better.

And these horns
are using this message and this power
to gain power over God's people,
and against the advancement of the Kingdom.
**The People of God are giving up hope
and giving in to the lies.**

March 4, 2020,
is the day everything changed.

The previous forty years
contained many events that were world shaking:
the AIDS epidemic,
the fall of the Berlin Wall,
the attack on the World Trade Center,
and the Global Financial Crisis.

But none of them had the sense of
before and after
like the day the world shut down.
For the first time in human history,
global commerce,
family life,
church,

education,
and
daily life,
stopped.
Everywhere.

In 2012,
when I first began writing
about the coming five hundred year shift,
I never truly imagined what was coming.
At that time, social media was a wave that was rising.
No one really foresaw a global surveillance state
like the ones imagined by
Aldous Huxley and George Orwell.
And no one expected that a government could one day
turn off all the bank accounts of its political opponents
like Justin Trudeau did in 2022.
No one believed that carefully crafted media
could be used to completely change the perceived
reality of people and nations,
and that real news and facts would be suppressed
as a means of control.

People are now waking up to the reality
we are not going back to normal.

The horns Zechariah saw
were not just armies.
Zechariah was seeing a global psychological war,
where lies and falsehood
would bombard people day and night.
And the result would be despair.

Both Lenin and Goebbels said a similar thing:
you only have to repeat a lie often enough
for it to become the truth.

For those of us who are committed to Jesus Christ,
there are days where the constant onslaught of lies
from the spirit of the age can become overwhelming.
We are living in the age that Zechariah saw.

Later on, I am going to talk in detail about the strategies
we need to use to fight this war.
Right now, we just need to recognize reality.

If you feel like the world around you is getting worse,
and you feel like you are losing hope for the future,
then maybe
it isn't you.

Do you feel like everything that you value
and believe is true
is under constant assault
day and night?
Maybe it isn't you.
Maybe you are feeling the pressure
of the messages
from the four horns.

Maybe there is something a lot larger going on,
and you are feeling the intense warfare of a global battle.
As I said earlier,
maybe this is not all about you,
and your calling as an artist.
God didn't call you
at this moment in time
for you.

God called you
to be a solution
to the problem.

The Solution

I mentioned earlier
God always sees the real problem.
In other words,
God looks for honesty and reality.
And then God creates a solution.

**In the Bible,
whenever the people of the Lord face a problem
the solution is always
a person.**

The first time we see this pattern clearly
is in the life of Joseph.
God calls Joseph to eventually deliver Egypt,
and then his family,
from famine.
Joseph preserves a people.
Moses is the answer God provides
to the cries of the Hebrew slaves.
He is the one God chooses to lead the people to freedom.
The pattern is most pronounced in the book of Judges,
where God raises up a deliverer
for Israel again and again.
God's solutions in Judges
took the names
Deborah,
Barak,

Samson,
Gideon,
and Jephthah.

Once a week, I gather with my prayer team
to pray for our community,
and for the global move of God
that is emerging in the arts.

We like to do "prayer experiments."
That is,
we pray for tangible things
that are real answers to prayer.
One of the rules for these experiments
is no "isms."

A lot of Christians tend to pray for
big,
vague,
and intangible things
that are safe,
but hard to measure.
The Bible never talks about
philosophical movements,
large, unnamed entities
or "isms."
The Bible is very specific.

Finding a solution for seven years of famine.
Getting a nation of slaves free from Egypt.
Freeing a nation from foreign oppression.
Restoring a people to their home.
Delivering humanity from sin and death.

In Zechariah, the problem is specific too,
even though at first glance,
the problem seems like an "ism:"
Global terrorism, "despairism," negativism.

No,
the problem is a global message
designed to keep God's people down.

It is a message connected to power,
and the powers of the world
are working in tandem,
using all the methods of communication possible
in a shared and continuous goal.

And what does God do?
Like the pattern in scripture,
the solution to the problem is human beings.
In the Kingdom,
the solution is always personal.
The solution is four artisans.

In most Bibles,
this word in Zechariah 1:20
is mistranslated.
Most use the word "smiths" or "blacksmiths."

It bears repeating
that the word here is the Hebrew word "Charashim."
As I mentioned earlier,
"charashim"
appears 35 times in the Old Testament.

In I Chronicles 4:14,
"charashim" is defined,
and then later translated into the Greek Septuagint.
This verse is a gift to us.
Because of it, we know how
the word was translated into the New Testament.

It is the word Artisan.

Words in the Bible are defined by their first appearance,
and so this word is defined by the life and experience
of Bezalel, the Master Artisan who built the Ark of the Covenant.

It is the word used for the Maker of the city
that Abraham is seeking
in Hebrews 11,
and it is the job that Joseph did

in Mark 6:3, when the people say,
"Isn't this Jesus, the son of the artisan?"

Remember what I said about the number four?
It represents the whole of creation.
So Zechariah
sees a global power.
And then Zechariah sees global artisans.
He doesn't see blacksmiths making weapons of war—
that is a mistranslation.
He sees artisans.

Zechariah is getting a little glimpse into a world
that he probably doesn't understand.
It is clear from the problematic language.
And with careful study,
it becomes clear that most translators
also do not understand what is going on.
That's why they didn't translate this accurately.
The original Hebrew is somewhat mysterious.

Zechariah sees a global power that makes everyone despair,
a global network of propaganda and messaging,
a barrage of images, sounds, words, and stories
that make people just keep their heads down and keep quiet.
He sees an endless twenty-four hour cycle of information
that is contrary to the word of God
and the hope of God's people.
He sees a round-the-clock message
that calls into question your nature as a human being:
a message that says good is evil
and wrong is right,
**a message that wants to destroy
everything good, true, and beautiful.**
That seems like science fiction.
Or does it?

Isaiah 55:8 contains
a piece of wisdom we should all consider:

**My thoughts are not your thoughts,
neither are my ways your ways, says the Lord.**

Many of us think that when we have a problem,
we need to come up with a human solution
and then ask God to bless it.

God's solutions are very different from ours.
And the Bible is a record of asymmetrical warfare.
Asymmetrical warfare
is when a war is fought between a conventional military force
and either a non-military force,
or a military force using extremely unconventional methods.

So in the Bible, we have a record of God
saving his people through some very unusual methods.
The army of Pharaoh was destroyed
when the Red Sea closed in on it.

Jericho fell
after the nation of Israel walked around the city for seven days,
and on the seventh day
they shouted and the walls came down.

Gideon led the nation to victory after
breaking pots,
flashing torches,
and blowing horns
with an army one-tenth the size of the enemy.

Jehoshaphat led the nation to victory
by sending the worship leaders into battle.

And the greatest victory of all
was won
by God taking the form of a servant,
embracing death on a cross,
and then, finally, rising again.

So Zechariah looks up,
and after seeing this global army of despair,
God shows him something else.
God shows him people,
but they are not soldiers in the conventional sense.
They are artisans.

All Hebrew words are very interesting.
First, the letters were originally derived from pictures,
and the pictures are arranged around a three letter root.
And if you look at these three letter roots,
often you can learn a lot about a word
by looking at the other words
on that word's "family" tree.

I noted we define a word in the Bible by the first use of it.
This is called the "Law of First Mentions."
The first use of charash, and the plural charashim,
is in Exodus 35.
This is in reference to Bezalel,
and all the artistic work
that was accomplished under his leadership.
So this is an artistic word.

Next, if we look at the words related to "charash,"
we see others,
spelled the same way,
with different vowels.
They are the words
"silent" and
"magic."

To the ancient Hebrew
there was a relationship
between the artisan,
quietness,
supernatural power,
and the priesthood.

**A war of ideas is not fought
the way a conventional war is fought.**
And Zechariah is filled with questions.

He asks the angel
what are these artisans here to do?
And the angel says
that the horns have arisen,
and no one can raise his head.

But these artisans have come,
and they are going to strike terror in the hearts of these horns.

**God is going to use an influx of creativity
to break the back of everything
rising up against God's people.**

God is going to bring terror
to those who are using fear as a weapon.

For every lie against the value and dignity of human beings,
a creative person is going to display the truth
with light,
color,
sound,
and movement.
And of course,
when necessary,
words.

So far, we have seen
that whenever there is a problem,
God raises up a person to be the solution.
God uses people as his primary weapon.
And we have also seen
that God's ways of warfare
are not our ways.
God specializes in asymmetrical warfare.
And in the vision of Zechariah,
God has chosen a specific group of people—
a group of artisans—
as his weapon for this global battle.

In the next section of this book,
we are going to look at the way we have thought of artists,
and how the definition of artist in the past
is changing.
We are going to explore three aspects of the artist
that are crucial for this moment:
The artist as listener,
the supernatural nature of creation,
and the artist as priest.

Then we will come back to this vision of Zechariah, and talk about the glory of God.

The Charashim

I've talked to many, many groups about
the call of God for the artist at this moment in time.
And when I use the word "artist,"
my audience immediately conjures up an image
of a young man
in an attic apartment.
It's cold,
and he is painting strange paintings
produced out of his tortured soul
that no one quite understands.
All he has to eat are tinned beans he warms up over a candle.
And yet,
he is driven by his need to create and express.
He is broke,
but comforts himself with his
other bohemian friends,
and his girlfriend, Mimi,
who happens to be dying of consumption in the adjoining room.
Cough,
Cough,
Cough.

If you didn't know,
that's the plot of *La Bohème*.

Yes,
it is a funny picture
but many people still hang onto the image

of the romantic, starving artist,
and somehow believe
this relates to what God is doing today.

Zechariah saw something much bigger
than an artist doing it for art's sake.

When I use the phrase
"army of artists"
and I talk about how God is raising up
artists and creative people for this time in history,
many assume
that I am raising up
a bunch of hippies
who sit in the back of church
(or in some radical places, up front)
and paint abstract pictures in pastel colors
while the worship band is playing
and call this activity "being prophetic."
And when the band stops,
the preacher gets up to do the really important thing:
talk.

This is not what Zechariah saw.
He saw Charashim.
He saw artisans as he understood them.

If we are going to talk about the artist in a time of war,
then we need to talk about the Bible's concept of the artist.

**We are living in a day when the concept of the artist
and the job of an artisan is quickly changing,
and the old notion of the starving artist is going away.**

The word "charash" first appears in the Bible
in Exodus 35:35.
And context is very important.
Most people have not seriously looked at this passage,
and so "Bezalel and Oholiab" have become two throwaway characters
next to more important people like Moses and Joshua.

A serious look at Exodus 35 through 38
gives us a very different picture,
and this picture is the first definition of artisan in the Bible.

What we see in the building of the Tabernacle
is a complex project site.
The leader of this project is Bezalel.
Twice we are told that Bezalel is filled
by the Spirit of God
to create and design all that Moses saw on the mountain.
He is given responsibility
for the creation of the worship center of Israel.
And his leadership is clear.
Bezalel is responsible for the oversight of the resources.
He is the one filled with the Holy Spirit,
and functions in many ways like a New Testament apostle,
imparting that spirit into the others under his leadership.
Bezalel is the one who makes the most important objects.
And Bezalel is given an assistant
whose role is to oversee
the people who will do the work of
weaving and tent-making.
Oholiab comes from the lowest tribe,
and is raised up
to assist and serve the larger project.

This model of a "workshop"
full of artisans creating objects
is similar to what we know about the ancient world.

There were no "artists" as we would understand them.

An artisan was a tradesperson
whose ability and skills always served a larger purpose,
and whose identity was often lost.
Ancient artisans were a nameless and faceless army,
and the work of creation was done in the name of
a king, pharaoh, or emperor.

What is unique about the Exodus story
is that Bezalel is named.
His assistant is named.

They are remembered.
God always honors those who work for him.

There are several references
and verses that I repeat.
I have done this in all of my books.
For over five hundred years, the role of the artist in scripture
was diminished,
and I find that even when I repeat myself,
people still revert back to the brainwashing.
So, if it seems like I am repeating myself,
I am.

Beyond the Bezalel story,
the concept of the artisan appears in many places.
In I Chronicles 4:14,
we are told that Israel had a "valley of the artisans,"
and this verse serves as a "Rosetta Stone."
It defines the word
and because of the Greek Septuagint translation,
we know how this word made its way into the New Testament.

In Proverbs 8:22-31,
God is described as the Master Artisan
and the process of creating the world
is similar to the process describing Bezalel's work in Exodus 36 and 37.

In II Chronicles, we see the artisan described again.
Hyram, the King of Tyre,
sends Solomon help to build the temple.

"Now I have sent a skilled man, endued with understanding, Huram-abi, the son of a woman of the daughters of Dan, and his father was a man of Tyre. He is trained to work in gold, silver, bronze, iron, stone, and wood, and in purple, blue, and crimson fabrics and fine linen, and to do all sorts of engraving and execute any design that may be assigned him, with your craftsmen, the craftsmen of my Lord, David your father.[14]

Again we are given clear descriptions
and these descriptions again echo Exodus 35.
Huram-Abi is trained to

work in precious materials.
He understands color;
he knows how to execute designs.
And there is an interesting detail:
He is half-Jewish,
and his mother is from the tribe of Dan,
just like Oholiab.

Throughout scripture,
we see these terms repeated:
skilled,
full of understanding,
able,
and trained.
All these are combined
so that the artisan could execute
any project he is assigned.

When we get to the New Testament,
things get really interesting.
In Mark 6:3
and Matthew 13:55,
our English Bibles say Jesus was called a "carpenter,"
and was the "carpenter's son."
But the word here
is the Greek word for charashim:
tekton.
Artisan.

The same word is used for the idol makers
making silver statues of Diana in Acts,
and it is the word used in Hebrews 11
for the Creator of the City Abraham was looking for.
And that city,
when it comes from heaven in Revelation 21,
is described using all the descriptors of both the work
of Huram-abi and Bezalel.

It is a city full of
gold,
color,
precious materials

and engraving.
It is a place crafted with exquisite skill.
And this place,
Jesus tells us,
is the place he has gone to prepare for us.

Tekton **is bigger than carpenter.**

Again,
this is the skilled master
who is able to oversee a project with precision
and design something
with the intent of executing it.

Jesus was an artisan.
And although we do not have any objects he made,
we know that he was a master storyteller
and teacher.
He was full of understanding and skill.
The army Zechariah saw,
was much broader and more profound
than a group of self-actualized,
self-expressive,
and self-motivated
artists.

He was seeing a group of highly skilled leaders
in every form of craft.

                                                          It was not about them.

Throughout most of history,
the artist was a member of a guild or a workshop.
It was not until the late Middle Ages
that we begin to see names
associated with artwork.
And even then,
the names are often associated with a school of a master artisan
or the workshop of a particular artisan.

When we get to the Renaissance,
the great names of Western Art begin to emerge.
Michelangelo,

Raphael,
and Da Vinci
all have a few things in common.

They were all trained in the workshop of another master.
They all mastered a body of skills
that were understood to be essential.
All three of these masters
painted,
drew,
designed costumes,
created architecture,
understood music and drama,
and had a vast knowledge of classical antiquity,
the Bible,
and theology.
All three oversaw workshops and had a body of
apprentices and assistants to create their monumental works.

Although this was not the primary role the artist played
after the Renaissance,
the idea that the artist
was a tradesperson
remained strong throughout history.

All this changed in the 19th Century.
Technological change,
especially photography and printing,
radically altered the artist's job.
The recording of events
and portraits
could now be done mechanically.
Images could be mass-produced.
It produced a crisis in the arts.

Along with this,
ideas from the Enlightenment and the
Romantic movement
began to influence art and artists.
In this environment,
the Impressionists emerged.
And it was out of them that the romantic concept of the artist

began to fix itself into our imaginations.
The scene I described at the beginning of this chapter,
is from Giacomo Puccini's opera
La Bohème,
"the bohemians."

Around this time,
the real force to redefine the artist appeared
with James McNeill Whistler.

In his book, *The Gentle Art of Making Enemies,*
Whistler recounts
how he took an art critic to court
and won.
In the book, Whistler describes the purpose of art this way:

> Art should be independent of all claptrap—should stand alone, and appeal to the artistic sense of eye or ear, without confounding this with emotions entirely foreign to it, as devotion, pity, love, patriotism, and the like. All these have no kind of concern with it; and that is why I insist on calling my works "arrangements" and "harmonies."[15]

**This definition has come to be known as
"Art for art's sake."**

Whistler said art was all about you,
and the artist began to be conceived as the
singular,
misunderstood,
solitary
genius.

Art became the expression of the artist,
for its own and the artist's purpose,
and whether or not it serves anyone is meaningless.
The only people who seem to understand
(or posture as if they understand)
are other artists and insiders.
And if you walk into any gallery today,
that word,
meaningless,

will come to mind.
My friend Ed Tuttle
was serving at a small art college
and he told me that the college was teaching the students that
all art is a form of catharsis.
"The trouble is," he said,
"catharsis is the Greek word for bowel movement.
That's what most of the art looks like."

If we are going to move forward
as an army of artists and artisans,
we have to redefine our place
in the world
and the Kingdom of God.
**The definition of artist
that has dominated the world,
cannot be the definition we use
when we talk about artists and artisans
for the Kingdom of God.**

The established definition is changing rapidly,
as the global art market
increasingly turns fine art into a commodity
that can be traded,
and technological development
rapidly disrupts what it means to be a creator.
We are going through a crisis
in the arts
just as dramatic as the invention of
photography and high speed printing.

**The artist in the Bible is a master at many crafts,
serves a larger purpose,
and that purpose always points to the Master Artisan.
The Biblical vision
always points to the City.**

In the next three chapters,
we are going to look at how the words
related to Charash
help us understand who and what an artist is at this time:

to be silent,
to be supernatural,
and to be a Levite.

Silence and Solitude

One word that has become more and more important
as I grow as a teacher and leader is
relationship.

The Kingdom of God is all about relationship.
And it should not surprise us that Hebrew
is a language that has
relationship
built into it.

Hebrew is a very interesting language.
Not only does it read right to left—
opposite of English—
but Hebrew letters can form pictures.
And unlike English,
all the words are built on three letter roots
and have a real relationship with one another.
Words in Hebrew
are like family trees
growing from common roots.

This language is relational.
So, for example,
there is a real relationship
between the words
for closeness,
for family,
and the word for sacrifice.

You can gain greater understanding
of a word or idea
by looking at the related words on the family tree.

Charash,
the word we are translating "artisan,"
some believe comes from a two letter root
that means "to cut."
In all the passages I quoted in the last chapter,
engraving is mentioned as one skill
that the artisan possesses.
To the ancient Hebrew,
cutting and engraving
were understood as essential skills for an artisan.

This makes sense in a world where the primary
visual art happened in stone.

There are several other words that share the three letter
root with charash.
The first word away from artisan on the family tree
is cheresh.
Cheresh can be translated
be quiet,
be deaf,
be secretive,
be cunning or crafty,
be deafening,
be imaginative.

Of course,
all of this usually can be understood in context.
As you saw from that list,
there are six English words that might be translated
based on context.
That is not unusual.
Context really is everything.
Bible translation is a process of making judgment calls,
and this is why you can have many variations
from one English translation to another.

Let's go back to this list.

Quiet.
Deaf.
Secretive.
Cunning or Crafty.
Deafening.
Imaginative.

If we could average out this list,
we get a sense of
silence and
solitude.

When people ask me what it is
that I do for a living,
I tell them I herd cats.

Cats are by nature independent.
Cats do their own thing.
Cats can be stealthy.
Cats can be very affectionate and purr.
Cats are often very quiet.
Cats can scratch if you scare them
or make them do something they don't want to do.
And cats can mark their territory
if they are insecure.

It is the same with artists and creative people.

**This army of artisans emerging
from the four corners of the earth
is very different
than what the church tries to make us.**
The church wants you to be out there evangelizing.
The church thinks you need to talk to strangers and be an extrovert.
The church wants you to conform.
The church wants you to be "under their covering."
All of these expectations
are counter to the nature of the artisan.
This is why so many artists
pull away from church
and try to do it themselves.
I know.

I have been there.

**Real artisans
do their best
when they pull away.**
The real act of creativity
happens in a secret place,
without distractions,
and without external stimulation.
It seems like a secret thing,
and then something emerges out of nothing.

And this relates to life in the Kingdom of God.

For us,
and our army,
we have to receive orders from the King.
The question I have been asked more than any other
over the past two decades is,
"How do I listen to God?"
The very first thing
you need to do
is be quiet.
You have to learn to quiet your soul,
calm your mind,
and wait and listen.
This is cheresh.
And in that quiet place,
the artisan
can hear the Voice of the Father,
and get inspiration.
It is in this quiet place
that new ideas form
and the imagination
begins to activate.
It is the place of learning to receive from God.

The four horns
are rising up across the earth
and they are deeply committed
to keeping you busy
and distracted.

The horns make
everyone's phone sound a high-pitched ping
to disturb your concentration,
and harden your soul to hear.
The horns keep you scrolling
so that your attention span shrinks to nanoseconds.
The horns keep you distracted with screens
and music that is too loud,
and cars playing hip-hop at a level that shakes the ground.
The horns create films full of violence and explosions
to harden and deaden your receptivity.

All of this
forms a callous on your heart
so that you cannot receive
a revelation from heaven.
And your mind becomes dull
and you become part of the problem
rather than a solution.

And to this raucous army with bright lights
and virtual reality,
God calls another group.
These warriors are different.
A lot of them are by themselves.
They have turned off the blurred screen
and the vibrating devices.
They have disconnected the cable
to the world, the flesh, and the devil.

And they are listening.

They are deaf to the world.
They are getting new ideas
and thinking for themselves.
They are thinking with God,
and getting in tune with the Mind of Christ
that is revealed to us in the Bible.
And when they do this,
they are disrupting
the mental stronghold
the horns are trying to build.

And one good idea
is food for a thousand.[16]

This is the ultimate in asymmetrical warfare.
Rather than harder, faster, louder,
this army is
smaller,
quieter,
simpler.

It's hard to bomb
a single person
quietly drawing pictures
in their studio.

It's a waste of resources
to send in a squadron
to take out
a solitary thinker.

This place,
the quiet place,
is the foundry
for the weaponry of the Kingdom.

We do not wage war against flesh and blood.
The weapons of our warfare are not carnal,
but are powerful in God,
for the pulling down of
mental constructs
and thought systems
and every high thing
that exalts itself above our Lord Jesus Christ.[17]

You are made to be different.
And part of this difference
is to recognize that the world system
is controlled by the enemy force.
It will only take you so far.

You are called and created to be different.

And that difference is by design.
You aren't going to fight like the enemy.
You are going to fight in the secret place,
where your heart and soul
are formed by the Voice of the Father.
And in that voice,
you will learn who He really is,
and who you really are.
And out of that secure identity,
you will begin to get new ideas
and new solutions.
And you will begin to create something
that is uniquely you.

This is the first branch on the artisan
family tree.
The next is also interesting:
Magic.

Magic

Artists
and creative people
are generally
tuned into the spiritual realm.

So,
the next branch of our
charashim
family tree
should not be surprising.

We are looking at words
that all stem from a root
that means
"to cut."
And the next word
sounds the same as "cheresh."
And it derives from
silence and secrecy:
magic,
magician,
incantation,
sorcery,
potions,
and
drugs.

**Pay attention that in both
Greek and Hebrew,
sorcery,
magic,
and drug use
are often synonymous.**
"Pharmokeia,"
the word behind "pharmacy"
in English,
is the word for "sorcery" in the New Testament.
The ancients made obvious connections
that we try to deny.

There is another important connection we need to understand.

We are so Christian
that we often forget
how the pagan world
works.

We think that
statues and idols
represent
a god.

At the time of the Bible,
an idol was not a symbol of a god.

**The idol
was
the god.**

This is why Exodus 20
in the Hebrew
connects worshipping other gods
and the making of graven (cut) images.
After the Reformation,
this commandment was purposely
divided in two
in order to forbid all making of art,
but to the ancients
it was understood:

if you worship another god,
you are going to make an idol.
In that world,
a statue was a god.

Isaiah 44 illustrates this in detail:

> How foolish are those who manufacture idols.
>   These prized objects are really worthless.
> The people who worship idols don't know this,
>   so they are all put to shame.
> Who but a fool would make his own god—
>   an idol that cannot help him one bit?
> All who worship idols will be disgraced
>   along with all these craftsmen—mere humans—
>   who claim they can make a god.
> They may all stand together,
>   but they will stand in terror and shame.
> The blacksmith stands at his forge to make a sharp tool,
>   pounding and shaping it with all his might.
> His work makes him hungry and weak.
>   It makes him thirsty and faint.
> Then the wood-carver measures a block of wood
>   and draws a pattern on it.
> He works with chisel and plane
>   and carves it into a human figure.
> He gives it human beauty
>   and puts it in a little shrine.
> He cuts down cedars;
>   he selects the cypress and the oak;
> he plants the pine in the forest
>   to be nourished by the rain.
> Then he uses part of the wood to make a fire.
>   With it he warms himself and bakes his bread.
> Then—yes, it's true—he takes the rest of it
>   and makes himself a god to worship!
> He makes an idol
>   and bows down in front of it!
> He burns part of the tree to roast his meat
>   and to keep himself warm.
>   He says, "Ah, that fire feels good."
> Then he takes what's left

      and makes his god: a carved idol!
He falls down in front of it,
   worshiping and praying to it.
"Rescue me!" he says.
   "You are my god!"
Such stupidity and ignorance!
   Their eyes are closed, and they cannot see.
   Their minds are shut, and they cannot think.
The person who made the idol never stops to reflect,
   "Why, it's just a block of wood!
I burned half of it for heat
   and used it to bake my bread and roast my meat.
How can the rest of it be a god?
   Should I bow down to worship a piece of wood?"[18]

Pay attention to the detail in this passage:
the words
craftsman,
blacksmith,
and carpenter
are all the same word in the Hebrew:
charash.

So this root "to cut"
makes sense.
How do you make an idol?
You cut or carve.
And at a base level,
if a person has the ability
to make a god,
that person has special powers.
That person has access to the supernatural
and they must be some sort of demigod themselves.

Maybe they are a magician,
or a sorcerer?

I talk about this in my book,
Bezalel: Redeeming a Renegade Creation.
Artisans,
blacksmiths,
and craftsmen

are all given unusual status
in the ancient world.[19]
We see this in the story of Bezalel,
where,
with careful study,
you see that parts of the story
have been removed.
And throughout time, Bezalel
goes from being a supernatural prophet
in Exodus 31,
to being written out of the story in Deuteronomy,
to being an architect over a worksite in Philo.
In the Talmud,
Bezalel becomes a thirteen year old boy
that Moses manipulates like a puppet.
By the Reformation,
Calvin removed the eight chapters about Bezalel from his commentaries,
and so Bezalel completely disappeared.

Today, typically, Christian artists will refer to
"Bezalel and Oholiab"
as a proof-text to support being an artist,
but nothing more.

Given the history of Israel,
and the long bent toward idolatry that didn't end
until the Second Temple period,
we can imagine
that Bezalel
may have been a problem.
Bezalel
is clearly given supernatural ability
by the Spirit of God
to create, lead, and teach.

**Every artist reading this knows
that there is an aspect of being a creator
that is supernatural and spiritual.**

Every skilled artist
has experienced that moment of inspiration

when the idea comes
out of nowhere.
And who hasn't finished a project
and stepped back
and discovered there are things
in it they didn't create?
**There is an element
in true creative activity
that is spiritual in nature.**

Recently, the Tate Modern Gallery in London
had an exhibition of the work of
Piet Mondrian and Hilma af Klint.
A member of our community
went to a private showing
and I was very curious about his thoughts.

"It was awful,"
he said.
"It was a big event promoting the occult."
I was curious, so
I went online to do some research.

It turns out,
Piet Mondrian,
one of my favorite artists,
received his inspiration from
famed occultist
Madame Blavatsky, and the Theosophists.
As for Hilma af Klint,
according to the Tate Modern website:

Both artists shared an interest in new ideas of scientific discovery, spirituality and philosophy. Af Klint was also a medium, and this exhibition showcases the large-scale, otherworldly paintings she believed were commissioned by higher powers.[20]

Graham Cooke
once said
"Satan is not looking for victims;
Satan is looking for allies."

**Nature abhors a vacuum,
and there is no art
that does not align itself spiritually.**
Human beings can create
without outside inspiration,
but that work will always be derivative.

It will be a diminishing shadow of what came before.
Just look at Hollywood and hip-hop,
that both now depend on "sampling"
from previous works.

We are dependent on an outside source.
That source
will either be God
and His endless release of growth and creativity;
or that source will be the world or the flesh,
creating echoes of what came before;
or the source will be the Devil.

There is no gray in the spiritual world.

And the demonic source
is a source of "discreativity."
It will ultimately rob, kill, and destroy.
This is the realm
of magic,
witchcraft,
and directed spiritual evil.
And one only has to go to a contemporary
art exhibit
to see open Satan worship,
demonically inspired art,
and people accessing the spiritual realm for new ideas.

One of the great myths
that developed after the Protestant Reformation
was the concept
of the sacred
and the secular.
Because of this,
many Christians in the arts

think their art has to be religious,
rather than formed by the Christian worldview.
The end product is a lot of bad art.

And in the public square,
things have to be "secular."
This produces meaningless art.
As we look around us,
those things that are made secular
by removing Christianity
quickly slip into paganism.

Paganism, at its root,
is the worship of the earth:
Erda or Gaia.
Second, it is the worship of fertility,
sex.
Look around you.

Public schools teach Buddhist meditation
in the name of "mindfulness,"
and yoga and Tai chi are practiced
in community centers
as a form of wellbeing.
And public art often openly
displays witchcraft
and occult symbols.

Derek Prince once said
that the "natural religion of man is witchcraft."
Simply put,
witchcraft, or paganism,
is the attempt to have power in the spiritual realm
and over other people
through control,
manipulation,
and domination.
You control things
in order to manipulate them,
with the end goal being domination.

Zechariah witnessed an artisan army that did not do this.

These tactics are the realm of the four horns.
Control,
manipulation,
and domination,
so no one can lift their heads.

**If you are an artist or creative person for the Kingdom,
you have to make a decision.**
From what well
are you going to draw
when you need water?

We live in an age of high-profile people
publicly renouncing their faith
and embracing the demonic in exchange for the glamour of evil.

The Faustian legend
is real,
and Jesus himself was offered all the kingdoms of this world
if he would just bow down to a fallen angel.
Yes, the enemy will give you promises,
but in the end
you are going to lose your soul.

In this war,
we have to remove every other source
that is not the Lord our God.
Worship the Lord your God,
and serve him only.[21]

That means
no consulting or dabbling in
tarot cards,
mediums,
horoscopes,
yoga,
eastern meditation,
or spiritual books that are not Christian.
Again,
there is no gray in the spiritual realm.
All truth is not God's truth,
because as Jesus himself told us:

Truth is a Person.

It means no
intoxication,
inebriation,
getting stoned,
blitzed,
or anything else that is going to alter your mental state.
These things all lower our defenses
or open us up to demonic influence.

Really.
There is a reason magic and drugs are linked.

It means aligning our physical bodies,
yes,
I mean sex,
with what the New Testament calls
basic Christian morals.
No sex outside a marriage between one man and one woman.

All these things
open us up to the influence
of the supernatural,
but close us off from the life of God.

Our spiritual lives have to be tuned
to the Kingdom
if we are going to make icons that point to the Lord.
Anything else
will open us up to making idols.
The war is real,
and dabbling near the edge
is dangerous.

Choose you this day
whom you will serve.[22]
In the next chapter,
we will look at the third word
that fills out the word Artisan:
Levite.

A Levite

If you read Hebrew,
you might be a bit perplexed
by the third word
related to *charash*.

The word for Levite
and the word for priest
are not on the charash family tree.

But if you read a Hebrew Lexicon
like *Brown, Driver and Briggs,*
or you use a concordance
like Strong's,
you will see this entry in the list of words:
"Cheresh, a Levite."

And in I Chronicles 9:15,
buried in one of the genealogies,
you will see
"Cheresh, a Levite who served the Tabernacle."
Here, "cheresh" is a proper name,
and the poor fellow was probably either deaf or mute.

The Levites who were not in the ranks of priests
served in the Tabernacle and in the Temple
as a resident army of musicians.[23]
And we can infer from the Psalms
that also meant singers, dancers, and instrumentalists.

Although there is not a direct word connection
between worship,
artisanship,
and priesthood
from the Hebrew root,
there is one for us and for our study.

The ancient world,
as we saw earlier,
understood the artisan as a mediator
between the physical and the spiritual world.
They made the unseen visible.

Zechariah was seeing an army in the future.
And the army of artisans he witnessed
was a group of New Covenant
artisans and creative warriors.
Saint Peter tells us
that in Christ,
through our baptism,
we have become part of a new house
built upon Jesus, the chief cornerstone,
and our role in that house is
a holy priesthood.[24]

**Our job is to offer spiritual worship to the Lord
and represent our Lord to the world.**
In fact,
this is the meaning of the word
"Christian:"
A little Christ.
A little anointed one.
And this implies
that we are anointed with the same Holy Spirit
that anointed and empowered Jesus.
We are a supernatural army of warriors,
who are joining in the ministry of Jesus
to overcome
the four horns.

As Peter continues in this chapter:
"You are a chosen race,

a royal priesthood,
a holy nation,
God's own people,
that you may declare
the wonderful deeds of him
who called you out of darkness
and into his marvelous light."[25]

The book of Isaiah ends
with a stirring vision
of the end of time.
The Lord gathers all the nations before him,
and he sees a multitude
of the nations and languages.
Missiologists would call these
the "people groups."

And beginning in Isaiah 66:19,
the prophet sees the process of
global evangelization.
Using every mode of transportation,
and every mode of communication,
the glory of the Lord is communicated
to the Gentiles.

And then the Lord will call all those who have
received him and his glory to the Mountain of the Lord,
and they will gather before him.
And then the Lord does something unexpected:

> And some of them
> also I will take for priests and for Levites, says the Lord.
> For as the new heavens and the new earth which I will make
> shall remain before me, says the Lord;
> so shall your descendants and your name remain.
> From new moon to new moon,
> and from sabbath to sabbath,
> all flesh shall come to worship before me,
> says the Lord.[26]

The book of Isaiah ends with God bringing all of his people
before him,

**and from among the Gentiles
God chooses priests and Levites.**

Although there will be no temple,
there will be worship.
And this worship will be
face to face and without a temple.
This worship will still require an army of priests who offer
and Levites who lead.

There is an eternal need for artists, artisans, and creators.

The battle we face,
and the war described in Zechariah
is ultimately a battle over worship.
This was the battle Jesus fought in the desert
when the fallen angel
asked God
to bow down
and worship him
in exchange
for all the nations of the world.

As we see here in Isaiah,
in the end,
Jesus is going to receive all the nations
who worship the Lord our God
and serve him only.
Satan wanted him to take a short cut
and submit like Adam.

Ultimately, it is all about worship.
Worship is not about songs
and a show on Sunday.
Worship is not about sermons or liturgies.
Worship is about your life,
about your body,
and about your service.

Choose this day
whom you will serve.

Let's go back to the terrifying vision
Zechariah sees
as God answers his prayer:
"Lord, what about us, what about Jerusalem,
what about God's people who are pressed down?"
And God shows Zechariah
a global army broadcasting a message.

And this broadcast is designed
to bring the people of God
to despair.
It is a message of lies and distortions.
And Jesus told us,
there is only one Father of Lies,
and so all lies originate from the same place.

This army
is not just a natural army,
but a demonically empowered,
supernatural army.
They are using lies,
magic,
and dark power to
bring God's people to a place
where no one can lift up his head.

And on the scene,
the Lord raises up another army.
These warriors are not screaming back.
They are not carrying guns.
They are not protesting or making a fuss.

They are quiet,
and they are listening to the Lord
and they are responding
by creating.
They are artisans who have become masters
in every craft,
and in the process
through their work,
and through their lives,
they have become

priests unto the Lord.
This is the ultimate
asymmetrical battle.
The artisans are not fighting the horns,
they are worshiping the Lord.

They have become clean vessels
as an offering unto the Lord.
Their bodies have been washed in pure water,
and the garments have been made white
like the priests of old,
not with the blood of bulls and goats,
but with the pure Blood of the Lamb,

Therefore are they before the throne of God,
    and serve him day and night within his temple;
    and he who sits upon the throne will shelter them with his presence.
They shall hunger no more, neither thirst any more;
    the sun shall not strike them, nor any scorching heat.
For the Lamb in the midst of the throne will be their shepherd,
    and he will guide them to springs of living water;
and God will wipe away every tear from their eyes.[27]

Before we end this section of the book,
I want to talk about the primary calling of the artisan in Zechariah
There is direction and purpose
in all of this.

God is calling you to a very strategic job.

Terror

On Sunday,
February 26, 1993,
I was in a van with my singing group
traveling outside New York City
near Fairfield, Connecticut.
I don't remember what we were listening to on the radio—
probably a hockey game—
when the broadcast was interrupted.

The World Trade Center in lower Manhattan was bombed.

Not long after the news came over the radio,
traffic stopped.
I don't remember how we got home that day,
but I remember it wasn't across the Bronx
like usual.

That day was just the beginning.
Eight years later,
they again tried to take down the World Trade Center,
and that time they succeeded.
Since then, there were the Paris attacks,
and the Boston bombing,
and other events
designed to make people afraid.
If you pick up any newspaper,
follow any news website,
or listen to any news channel on television,

it will not take long for you to feel anxious
and afraid.

Fear is the commodity of our time.

Zechariah 1:20 is difficult in the Hebrew,
and the English translations often are not much help.
Here is my paraphrase:

> Zechariah asked,
> "What are these artisans coming to do?"
> And the angel replied,
> "These are the powers that have scattered Judah;
> everyone is so depressed that they are hanging their heads.
> But these artisans have come
> to strike terror in the hearts of the horns—
> the powers of the nations,
> and they have come to cast down the power of the nations
> that have come to strike terror in God's people."

God is raising up artisans
to terrify the terrorists.

While I was making my morning coffee,
I looked over the weekend Observer.
The cover story
was about an international financial scandal
with a bank
already involved
in closing people's bank accounts
to silence free speech.
There was a feature article about coping with isolation and loneliness.
The entertainment section featured an interview
with an actor who plays a sexy Catholic priest on TV
who also makes homosexual romance movies.
And of course, there was the usual list of
mayhem,
violence,
corruption,
and iniquity
that makes up the daily news.
This wasn't an unusual weekend newspaper;

this was average.
If you consume a regular diet of this,
I promise you
it will make you depressed,
angry,
or both.

The powers of the nations
seem to be committed to
what we see in Psalm 2:

> Why are the nations so angry?
> Why do they waste their time with futile plans?
> The kings of the earth prepare for battle;
> the rulers plot together
> against the Lord
> and against his anointed one.
> "Let us break their chains," they cry,
> "and free ourselves from slavery to God."[28]

It seems that the whole world is committed to waging war against God,
against Jesus,
against Israel,
against Judeo-Christian civilization,
and against righteousness in all forms.

And the Lord responds:
But the one who rules in heaven laughs.
The Lord scoffs at them.
Then in anger he rebukes them,
terrifying them with his fierce fury.[29]

Again
we see this word
terror.
But also, laughter.

God is going to do something completely different.

In heaven,
there is laughter,
even if
on earth,
there is fear and terror.
God is about to release a revelation of joy.

I've spent most of the past two decades
sitting
with artists and creative people
and listening
to their stories,
and helping
them walk into healing.

There is very little that shocks me anymore.
I've heard horrendous tales of abuse and neglect.
I've listened to stories of churches and leaders
knowingly taking advantage
of artists in every way possible.
I've heard stories of
false accusations,
lies,
addictions,
and tragedies.
And I have seen many, many people
get free from all of it and get released into a new level
of wholeness and creativity.
One thing is clear.
If you are an artist or a creative person,
Satan hates you.

Our enemy cannot create or reproduce.
He can only stop you from creating or reproducing.
And he can rob, kill, or destroy your creativity.
The enemy and his hordes can get you to quit.
That's all.

And again,
God has chosen you to be the secret weapon.
He has given you an ability to see,

hear,
smell,
and experience
the sounds and sights of heaven.

This is the quiet place.
He has given you the ability
to translate what you receive into something others,
who are much less gifted,
can also encounter.
**You can make the reality of the Kingdom of Heaven
available to others.**
And in a world that is becoming
a little more like hell
every day,
that little glimpse of heaven
is enough to strike terror
into the hearts of Satan's empire.
Those who create fear in others
are really very afraid themselves.
And it is all an illusion,
because in an ugly world,
even a little child
and a fool knows what beauty is.

**A glimpse of light in the gray, dim streets of the city
can light up a whole neighborhood.**

This is why,
whenever evil regimes appear,
they do the same thing:
They break beautiful things and replace them with meaningless ones.
They destroy monuments and statues.
They burn libraries.
They either limit creative people through censorship,
brainwashing, or drugs,
or they round them all up and kill them.

What are they afraid of?
A free imagination is a very dangerous thing.

The American Civil War was the deadliest
war the United States has fought to date.
In the war and the resulting end of Southern slavery,
the battle of ideas was won

by two Christian women:
Harriet Beecher Stowe and Julia Ward Howe.

Harriet Beecher Stowe
was sitting in church
and prayed that God would help her do something
that would be as influential as her brother,
Henry Ward Beecher, the most famous preacher in America.

As she prayed,
she saw a vision,
inspired by a recent visit to Kentucky
and her first hand encounter with slavery.
That vision became the novel,
Uncle Tom's Cabin.

Julia Ward Howe,
at the start of the Civil War heard a group of soldiers
singing the folksong,
"John Brown's Body lies a-mouldering in the grave."
She was asked to write a better set of words,
and the lyrics came to her in bed, just before she went to sleep.
She penned the words of what would become
the Battle Hymn of the Republic.

Mine eyes have seen the glory of the coming of the Lord;
He is trampling out the vintage where the grapes of wrath are stored;
He hath loosed the fateful lightning of His terrible swift sword:
His truth is marching on.

I have seen Him in the watch-fires of a hundred circling camps,
They have builded Him an altar in the evening dews and damps;
I can read His righteous sentence by the dim and flaring lamps:
His day is marching on.

I have read a fiery gospel writ in burnished rows of steel:
"As ye deal with my contemners, so with you my grace shall deal;"

*Let the Hero, born of woman, crush the serpent with his heel,
Since God is marching on.*

*He has sounded forth the trumpet that shall never call retreat;
He is sifting out the hearts of men before His judgment-seat;
Oh, be swift, my soul, to answer Him! Be jubilant, my feet!
Our God is marching on.*

*Glory, Glory, Hallelujah!
Glory, Glory, Hallelujah!
Glory, Glory, Hallelujah!
Our God is marching on.*

**These women fought with the tools
of revelation
and imagination.**
They were able to instill in others
the moral evils of slavery,
and the vision of the army of the Lord.
And in doing this,
they were able to put these ideas into others.

**Revelation and imagination
are our most powerful weapons.**

When you help people see and imagine
something better,
they get a glimpse of what's possible.

Terrorism
is all about removing possibilities
and making people afraid.
And people who are afraid,
will do stupid things
and make bad decisions.
Scared people are easy to control.

And to this situation
God laughs and sends a bunch of people
telling good stories,
singing powerful songs,
and making beautiful things.

And here and there,
people who are laughing in the face of fear.

In Luke 4, Jesus read from Isaiah 61
and said it was part of his calling as the Messiah.
At the core of his mission as the Messianic King
are these words:

To all who mourn in Israel,
he will give a crown of beauty for ashes,
a joyous blessing instead of mourning,
festive praise instead of despair.
In their righteousness, they will be like great oaks
that the Lord has planted for his own glory.
They will rebuild the ancient ruins,
repairing cities destroyed long ago.
They will revive them,
though they have been deserted for many generations.[30]

God is not going to fight against fear and terror
with more fear and terror.
That's the world's way, not the Kingdom.
God's plan for destroying the horns of the nations
is positive.

Beauty for ashes,
Joy for mourning,
praise instead of despair.

God is raising up
those who will be part of a
great rebuilding.
And this is the opposite of the plan
to rob, kill, and destroy.

Can you hear the prosperity and blessing in this?
This is not just about finances,
this is about being a conduit of the resources of heaven.
The artisans in Zechariah
are called to walk up to an army
that is designed to make everyone

poor,
depressed,
afraid,
and immobilized,
and be
life,
light,
joy,
abundance,
and creativity.

And the resources we use
come from heaven.
Our supply is eternal,
and our weapons are mighty in God
to tear down all the strongholds,
arguments,
and human pride
that exalt themselves above God.

This is how we strike terror in the hearts of the terrorists.

If God calls you into a battle,
the purpose of the battle is victory.
In the next chapter,
we are going to look at the victory
God promises
for the army of artisans.

A City Without Walls

Earlier this year,
I went on an unusual prayer journey.
God was speaking to me about the
orphan spirit over London.
Part of that journey
led me to all the places where
the Romans abandoned Britain.
I traveled to the City of London,
to Colchester,
and to York.
And everywhere I went,
I found the same thing:
a hole in the wall.

When you listen to God
and go on a journey with Jesus,
often, you discover things that you never expected.
My journey took me to several places
where there was a breach in the wall.
The Romans left places unprotected,
and where these gaps were left,
the Vikings would spend the next few centuries
terrorizing the local populations.

In the ancient world,
a wall served as protection.
But it also served as a boundary
between cultures,

and as a demarcation
between different languages
and value systems.
For the most part,
in our world,
the walls we erect are in our minds.
They are boundaries created through
philosophies,
thought systems,
political grids,
or governments.
Of course,
we are also seeing places on earth
where we once again need physical walls.

Remember at the beginning of this book
when I said that God told Zechariah
the goal
was prosperity.
We are now on the other side of that vision.
Zechariah sees a man with a measuring line.

At the end of the Bible
John also describes an angel with a measuring line in Revelation 21.
And both are doing the same thing:
measuring Jerusalem.

And in the midst of this vision,
Zechariah is told to proclaim a message:

> Jerusalem shall be inhabited as villages without walls,
> because of the multitude of men and cattle in it.
> For I will be to her a wall of fire round about,
> says the Lord,
> and I will be the glory within her.[31]

Unlike the Romans,
who only saw the local Britons
as a population to use and rule,
and then abandon as orphans,
the Lord sees Jerusalem
as a city invested with his presence.

And he sees an unlimited population
drawn to him
in the city.

And the Presence of God—
his personal dwelling in their midst—
becomes the protection.

**God is the boundary
and God is the protection.**

No longer do they need a physical wall,
and so many people are drawn to the Presence
that the place can no longer be contained by walls.

The Presence of God,
and the Glory of God
becomes the wall of fire around this city.

The culture of this new place
is caught up not in activity,
not in outward cultural values,
not in practices or even genetic similarities.
No.
This city is defined
by a **relationship** with the God who dwells there.

As John would tell us at the end of the book,
there is no temple in this city.
The gates are open day and night,
and the kings of the nations bring their glory into this city.[32]

This is a place protected by the glory of God.
The world rises up to make war against
Judah,
Jerusalem
and all God's people.
The plan is to bring despair
in order to cause us to quit.

"Let's just quit.
This battle is too hard

and I have been at this too long,
and I don't seem to ever get a break.
Maybe it's time to give up."

And then there is a song
coming over the mountains.
It is the song of the redeemed.
It is the song of children
and fathers,
and the song of those who are clean.
This is the song of the artisans.
This is the sound of light,
color,
movement,
joy,
hope,
and peace.

These warriors are not using tanks.
They are not cutting off heads,
or running through residential neighborhoods
trying to kill old ladies and children.

No, this army
is far more terrible.
They are changing the thoughts and beliefs of those who hear.
They are shifting the message
from one of death and destruction
to one of life.
Nothing shall separate you from the Love of God.

All things are possible
for those who believe.

Jerusalem
shall be inhabited
as a city without walls,
where the glory of God dwells within
and the fire of God surrounds.

This is about the Kingdom.
It looks to a day when all things will be made right.

But it also looks to now.
I am not spiritualizing this text.
Paul told us
that we are the temple of the Holy Spirit.[33]
If you are in Christ,
then this City,
in part,
is inside you,
and you are to be a glory bearer.
And from the inside out,
your creative energy becomes the fire all around.

The presence of God in you,
little creator,
is the engine of victory in a global war.

We have just walked through the vision Zechariah
had for the end of time.

Now let's look at another place in scripture
that describes the time we live in.
We can't understand our place in the battle
until we understand the transition we are experiencing.

In the next section, we are going to look at another shift in time,
much like the one we are in right now.
And in order to understand our place as warriors and artisans,
we need to dig deep into the greatest warrior in the Bible.
It so happens that he, too, was an artist:
David.

Part II

DAVID

The Generation of the Sons of Eli

In 1988,
I received
my first
prophetic word.

I was seventeen years old,
and at the time
did not understand what I was
hearing:

> **The Generation
> of the Sons of Eli
> is coming to an end.**

I have lived with this word
for over thirty-five years.
God has spoken to me about this many times since then,
and I have reflected deeply on its meaning,
and the origins of the phrase
in the first book of Samuel.

Most of all,
it has helped me understand the times we live in:
we are in the Generation of the Sons of Eli.

In order to understand the role
of the artist and artisan
presented in the vision of Zechariah,
we need to understand the cycle and direction of time.

Zechariah was witnessing a war
that happened
when the cycle of time
and the larger direction of time
collide.
It is a unique moment.

In my book
An Army Arising,
I described the details of the "Five Hundred Year Shift"
that the church,
and the larger culture
experiences.
In that book,
I described it as a change in the questions
that people are asking.
So, for example,
the question five hundred years ago was
"What must I do to be saved?"

That question is now surpassed by a new fundamental question:

Who am I?

We are living through **a collective identity crisis.**
From this question,
two other questions have emerged:

Do I have value?

This question arose after
the shift away from a Judeo-Christian worldview
to one rooted in "Darwinistic" thinking.
If I evolved from nothing,
for no apparent reason,
then
what value do I have
other than to
buy stuff,
have sex,
and make money
before I become food for worms?

This leads to a world where only the strong survive.
And it has led to an identity crisis.

People don't know where they came from
and so they don't know who they are.

And the next question follows these other two.
If you don't know where you came from,
and you don't know who you are,
then you don't know where you belong.
And this sense that "I have no place to belong"
is resulting in a global migration of people
looking for a better country.

And when these migrants and refugees get there,
they discover that the
unanswered questions:

Do I have value?
Who Am I?
Where do I belong?

continue to haunt them like a specter in the night.

This shift is now being noted by a number of writers and thinkers.
We are in it,
and it is happening all around us.

Phyllis Tickle,
in her book *The Great Emergence,*
pointed out that this phenomenon
is not just a Christian one,
but a Judeo-Christian one.
She points to the reforms that happened under David
as an example.[34]

Going back through the past four thousand years,
every five hundred years,
God's people go through a housecleaning of sorts.
Old things get shaken up,
and new things are birthed.
We are going through the shaking and birthing right now.

These periods are violent,
destructive,
and very creative.

And this shifting and shaking
is the cause
and also the theatre
of the war we are experiencing.

And this leads us back to the Sons of Eli.

The first book of Samuel
opens with a domestic drama.
Like a lot of families,
the holidays bring up all the underlying problems.
Elkanah has two wives.
One of them has many children
and the other,
Hannah,
has none.

And each year,
when they go to Shiloh to sacrifice,
Hannah only gets enough food for herself,
and the other wife, and all her children,
receive a feast.
Because of her barrenness,
the other wife and her children mock Hannah.

The setting of our drama is
the leaderless state of Israel.

Eli,
the High Priest, is in his nineties,
and he has been a judge over Israel for seventy years.
The Judges were the ad hoc leaders of Israel
that provided unstable leadership for the nation.
There was no succession from one to another,
and they varied a lot in quality.
This period in Israel is summed up
in one sentence:
"And everyone did what was right in their own eyes."[35]

Sound familiar?
When I talk with thinking people,
they look around the world,
and they point out there are no true leaders
in any of the nations,
institutions,
or churches.
A leader presents vision,
and when there is no vision,
the people cast off restraint.

Eli's sons,
Hophni and Phineas,
presided over the remains of the Tabernacle
of Moses at Shiloh.

The Sons of Eli
are described in the Hebrew as
"Sons of Belial."
Evil is personified.
In English, it is usually translated "worthless,"
but let's assume
that Belial describes a being.
The Sons of Eli
were sons of the devil,
and they were also the gatekeepers of the worship of Israel.

The old adage
"familiarity breeds contempt,"
is true.
The Sons of Eli
were close to holy things
although they were not holy themselves.
And because of this,
they thought they could take the best offerings for themselves.
They thought they could sleep with the women
who presented themselves
as volunteers in the Tabernacle.
And they had thugs who took advantage
of those who came to worship
and forcibly took the offerings from the worshipers.

They believed that since they were in charge,
there would be no consequences for their actions.

And although
he warned his sons,
Eli was permissive,
and did not stop them.
Eli was lax and corrupt as well.
Eli himself was sleeping in the Tabernacle,
and he instructed the child Samuel
to sleep in the Holy of Holies.

The family of Eli
first and foremost
had
no
fear
of God.
Let's take a pause right here.

The worship of Israel
that was established to be a model of heaven on earth
has apparently become hopelessly corrupt.
It had become a center of commerce,
and a center of sexual immorality.

Remember the road in the wilderness?
Artists and artisans recognize the times they live in,
and some actually are prophetic forerunners.

The church in our day
is much like the Sons of Eli.
This is a "come to Jesus" moment,
and I am going to be very blunt.
The things I am saying
come from over thirty years of ministry experience.
I have worked backstage at charismatic conferences,
within the structures of two mainline denominations,
and in several para-church organizations.

Much of the church
holds holy things with contempt,
and does whatever is right in its own eyes.

There is no fear of God.
Those in leadership believe that the rules can be changed or bent to their liking.
Others believe that the rules belong to the little people and not to them.
There are obvious examples
like the Roman Catholic "Synod on Synodality"
and the global Anglican Realignment,
but there are many other, similar things going on all over.

Because of career luck, I guess,
I am a first hand witness to "the back of the puppet stage."
There is a lot of money in religion.
At the time of Eli,
the system became commercial.
At the time of Jesus,
the system became commercial.
At the time of the Reformation,
the system became commercial.

All you need to do is a search on
church growth,
worship leading,
and Christian music,
and the signs are obvious.
The church is becoming commercial.

I have personally seen leaders take the best offerings for themselves.
I have witnessed others use their power and charisma
to take sexual liberties with whomever was available.
I have watched conferences become money-making operations.
For many,
the worship of the All Holy God, blessed be He,
is now just one arm of the entertainment industry:
a form of show business.
God's people are just the potential consumers of more content.

I have witnessed divorce and adultery among bishops and pastors
get laughed off as "boys will be boys,"
while those who struggle to live holy lives with same-sex attraction
receive harsh and unmerciful punishment.

I have witnessed denominations punish
good, holy, faithful men
for not going along
with heresies and false doctrines,
and I have watched leaders
call evil good and good evil
again and again.

And somehow,
over my thirty year career,
the evil seem to never see justice.

I have witnessed first hand that the most dangerous thing
to people and the church
is an evil, ignorant fool.

Somehow,
in the last sixty years,
all the standards have been inverted.
Although the sexual crazy is obvious,
there are multitudes of other ways
where everyone does
whatever is right
in their own eyes.

And like Israel of old,
idols and other gods
seem to be no problem
for the people of God.
And when these issues come up,
the answer seems to always be,
"Who are you to tell me what to do?"

Most troubling
is the number of Christians
who have embraced yoga.
When one assumes the positions in yoga,

you are attempting to mimic the shape of a god,
and in doing so,
the demon this god represents is given access to your body.
And the purpose of this is to increase your sexual energy.
When I have talked with Christians who practice yoga,
They tell me they have a hard time hearing God
and their sense of right and wrong is diminished.
And oddly,
when someone is confronted about this,
they usually go into a ferocious rage.
Yoga cannot become holy.
This is not the Holy Spirit.

One aspect of my ministry is inner healing and deliverance.
My opinions about yoga were formed
when I came face to face with demons
who would not come out of suffering people.
There is no gray area in the spiritual realm.

One day an elderly woman pulled me aside.
With tears in her eyes,
she told me how her
church based senior citizen center
invited her to a wellness program.
It was based on yoga,
and she was pressured to participate.

"I am so ashamed.
They made me worship these other gods,
and I have grieved the Holy Spirit."

We have lost the basic sense of holiness
that previous generations took for granted.

We have forgotten
that our bodies are not our own.
We were bought with a price:
the precious blood of Jesus.

As I said at the beginning of this book,
It's not about you.

We are living in a time
much like the beginning of the books of Samuel.
The world is leaderless,
the church is
financially,
morally,
and theologically corrupt,
and there are enemies all around.

Let's take a pause.
There is therefore no condemnation
for those who are in Christ Jesus,
for the law of the spirit of life in Christ Jesus
has set you free from the law of sin and death.[36]

If you feel conviction,
tell it to the Lord,
and go find a friend, and tell them.

Now back to our story.

Meanwhile,
back at Shiloh,
our little domestic drama
continues.

As I said earlier,
God solves a problem
by sending a person.
Hannah's problem
is Israel's problem.
She has no heir,
and the nation has no leader.

Hannah is a prophetic metaphor
for the whole nation.
She is barren,
and she is being mocked by everyone around her.

In her pain,
Hannah cries out to God,
and that cry is heard,

and she gives birth to a son.
The most creative act of heaven is the birth of a child.
And Hannah's song of joy would point to Mary
and her child,
Jesus.

"My heart exults in the Lord,
my strength is exalted in God."

Her answer is Samuel,
and like Mary,
she would surrender her son to God,
and leave him at the temple.

And this little boy would see the realities of the priesthood under Eli.
And he would grow,
like Jesus,
in stature, and favor, with God and men.

Whenever God does something,
first he speaks.
God's voice is the engine of creation.

God sends a man of God to Eli
who is not from Shiloh.
He is living away from the system.
And he comes and gives a word of judgment.
God is going to take away the birthright of the Levites,
destroy the house of Eli in one day,
and create something new:

> And I will raise up for myself a faithful priest, who shall do according to what is in my heart and in my mind; and I will build him a sure house, and he shall go in and out before my anointed for ever.[37]

In 2007, I was at a regional gathering of leaders in Northeast Ohio.
I went because the prophet Bob Jones
was going to speak to this group,
and I wanted to hear what he had to say.
Belonging House had just begun,
and I was looking for encouragement.

Bob looked over the group and said,

"You all had words that God was going to
begin the great end-time harvest here.
He promised you that you would carry the glory.
But you have touched the glory,
and the Lord says he is moving on.
Some of you took offerings for yourself,
and others of you built your ministries
on the anointing.
You touched the glory.
And so the Lord says he is not going to use you.
Some of you are going to lose your buildings,
and some of you are going to get very sick.
And others of you are going to lose your congregations.
But God has his eyes on others,
and some of you are going to see God use you,
and you are going to know that this word is for you.
Whenever it snows,
God will show you that something good is about to happen."

Well, that was quite a word.

And the leaders in the group,
oddly,
went on as if nothing happened.
And several of them lost their buildings,
several got very sick,
and others lost everything.

A few months later,
I took a small group to Kentucky for Easter,
and we found ourselves in a freak snowstorm.
It had been a warm, sunny day
just hours before.
And one of the folks in our group
poked me and said,
"Remember that word from Bob Jones?
Maybe it was for us."

This was a heavy chapter.
And it is as serious as a heart attack.

If you are called to this moment in time,
you need to recognize things for what they are.
**The Generation of the Sons of Eli
is coming to an end.**
And the Sons of Eli are not going without a fight.
They are using algorithms,
credentials,
layers and layers of middle-men
and fact-checkers,
surveillance,
and social pressure
to keep a grip on power.
War is hell.

**This is part of the process
of building something new.**

Are you going to be part of the spirit of the age,
or walk in a different spirit?
Paul promised us that if we are filled with the Holy Spirit,
we have the power in us
of the age to come.[38]
We do not have to be sons of Belial.
We can walk into this world
not in agreement with the generation of the Sons of Eli.
We can be sons and daughters of God.

It's scary,
but it is for a larger purpose.

In the next chapter, we are going to look at
another part of the process of the Five Hundred Year Shift:
the point of no return...

The Point of No Return

In every five hundred year shift,
there is a moment of no return.
You have gone from one era in human history to another.

In the last five hundred year shift,
it was the moment at the Diet of Worms
when Martin Luther said he would not recant.
Another was the moment
Rome fell.
For us,
it is clear
we are not going back to the world before
September 11, 2001,
or March 4, 2020.
Those worlds are gone.

These are no-turning-back moments
when everything changes.

Although we don't know the date,
the Five Hundred Year shift in I Samuel
also had a no-turning-back moment.

After Hannah gives her son to Eli as an offering to God,
Samuel is made to sleep in the Holy of Holies.
And God speaks to him.
Out of his time in the Presence of God,
Samuel is established as a prophet in Israel.

His first prophetic word as a child
is the destruction of the House of Eli.
Whenever God brings about a big shift,
he first establishes
someone who can bridge the transition.
Samuel is the last judge,
and also a prophet.
Samuel rises up as the bridge between two eras.

And then the no-turning-back moment happens.

Eli's sons,
Hophni and Phineas,
take the ark out of the Tabernacle,
and into battle.
The Philistines,
the arch-enemy of Israel throughout this period,
defeat the armies of Israel
and the ark is **taken into captivity.**

In one day,
the ark is captured,
Hophni and Phineas die,
Eli dies,
and the wife of Phineas dies in childbirth.
Her son is named "Ichabod."
Literally,
unglory.
The glory of God is gone.
The family and leadership of Shiloh ends.
From this point on,
worship in the Tabernacle is permanently changed.
There is no going back to the period of the Judges.

The ark,
the focus of Israel's worship
first goes into exile,
wreaks havoc in a pagan temple,
and then is returned to Israel.
It will be cared for by Eliezar
for twenty years.

Before the new thing can emerge,
the old thing has to stop.
Israel had to come to terms with the facts:
the temple at Shiloh
has no leaders,
and the ark is gone.
Things have changed.
And the ark is never going back
into the Tabernacle of Moses.

Samuel steps in
and the first thing he asks the people to do
is give up their foreign gods
and stop doing whatever is right in their own eyes.[39]

Before we can move forward into the new thing,
we have to do the same thing.

As Joshua asked the people,
choose you this day whom you will serve.[40]

I lead a large and diverse group of people.
They are artists in all different forms.
I understand that you need to be unique,
independent,
and creative.
But,
if you are called to be an artisan for the kingdom,
you have to submit to the King
and the Kingdom.
This means you have to align your life
with the clear teaching of Jesus and the Bible.
Let's start with
do unto others
as you would have others
do unto you.[41]

Many of the artists I talk with
do not know the Bible well enough
to know when they are out of alignment.

**You will not hear God clearly
until you learn how God speaks in the Bible.**
The end of this book will give you practical ways to hear God.
God never contradicts his own revelation.

So Samuel calls the people back to God,
and he becomes the last judge.
But,
as we have seen,
the old way is no longer working,
and Samuel's sons
are as bad as the Sons of Eli.
There is no going back.

There is no temple.
There is no ark.
There is no priesthood.
And now there are no judges.
And the people cry out for a king
just like the other nations.

I mentioned in the last chapter
that there was a prophet who came and prophesied
that there would be a new priesthood.
This is another no-turning-back moment.

There is a point in transition
that is chaotic
and painful.
That is the reign of Saul.
He is not the answer,
but the **first step** toward the new thing.

Saul is the next step on the road toward a worship revolution.
He is not the revolution,
and it can be argued from the promises
on the tribe of Judah,
that he was never intended to establish a dynasty.
But someone had to be first,
and he was.

The other day, I was walking through the streets of London
with a member of our community.
She was unaware
of the cataclysmic changes that have happened to London
in the past five years.
As we talked, it was clear to me
that this is the **way things are now.**
I could resist them and try to go back to the past,
or I could step into them.

In recovery, we say a prayer that you probably know:

> God, grant me the serenity
> to accept the things I cannot change,
> the courage to change the things I can,
> and the wisdom to know the difference.

Part of coming to the no-turning-back moment
is to **accept** this reality.
We are not going to undo
what happened in the past few years.
The entire world has been changed.
We can't go back to the past by becoming a Calvinist
or attending a Latin mass.

> We have to accept that we have passed the point of no return.

We live in Babylon,
and we can either live like refugees,
or we can be like Daniel and Esther, who overcame.

Once you accept things for how they really are,
then you can decide what needs to change.

An amazing thing I have discovered
is that when you decide the direction of your heart,
and align it with God,
then the wind of heaven gets behind you
and moves you to where you need to be.

Aligning Your Heart

Have you noticed that the road through the wilderness
is going decidedly downhill?

This intense movement is part of the process.
It is slow, and meditative,
and introduces intense themes.

We cannot get to the mountain of the Lord
without going through the valley of tears.

Israel is in trouble.
Samuel is old.
The temple is gone.
The ark is at someone's farm.
The nation is surrounded on all sides
by enemies.
And Samuel's sons
are no better than the Sons of Eli.
The system of Judges
never worked,
and there is no going back.

Israel cries out for a king,
and Samuel
obeys.
Saul is the greatest example
of the kind of leader everyone wants.

Saul is tall and good looking.
Saul seems to do the right things at the right moment.
Saul is the best example of the firstborn.
He steps in and creates a kingdom
out of nothing.
But deep down inside,
his heart is really far from God.
He too does whatever is right in his own eyes.

And it doesn't take long for Samuel
to realize that Saul lacks character.
And, as in so many places in the Bible,
the issue comes down to worship.
Saul decides to offer sacrifice
as if he were a priest.

And out of this, Samuel condemns him:

> And Samuel said to Saul, "You have done foolishly; you have not kept the commandment of the Lord your God, which he commanded you; for now the Lord would have established your kingdom over Israel for ever. But now your kingdom shall not continue; the Lord has sought out a man after his own heart; and the Lord has appointed him to be prince over his people, because you have not kept what the Lord commanded you."[42]

Jesus tells us in John 4 that the eyes of the Lord
scan to and fro over the whole earth
seeking those that will worship the Father
in Spirit and in truth.[43]

It is all about worship.

And God begins to look for another king.

Saul again offers sacrifice on his own,
and disobeys the Lord,
and Samuel again condemns him:

> "Has the Lord as great delight in burnt offerings and sacrifices,
>   as in obeying the voice of the Lord?

> Behold, to obey is better than sacrifice,
>   and to hearken than the fat of rams.
> For rebellion is as the sin of divination,
>   and stubbornness is as iniquity and idolatry.
> Because you have rejected the word of the Lord,
>   he has also rejected you from being king."[44]

Yes,
I know this is a book for artists and creative people.
In all my books, I repeat a version of the same statement:

**Your inner life determines your creative output.
It is all about who and what you worship.**

We are all like Isaiah.
I am a man of unclean lips
and I live among a people of unclean lips.
[45]
Before we can get to the good part,
we have to look at our hearts.
The current social media environment,
the current church culture,
and the current arts world
all value the same things:
good looks,
a good show,
and a big platform.
This isn't new,
it was here three thousand years ago.
Human nature is always human nature.

God does not take delight
in you doing
heroic things
for him
that look good
to everyone else.

This is why leaders get into trouble.
They build things without God,
and then find themselves personally vulnerable.

Right here we see the foundation:
listen to God and do what he tells you.

And the next two phrases are especially important to
artists and creative people:
rebellion is like witchcraft,
and stubbornness is like idolatry.

Arty people go against the flow.
I understand that.
I do it.

The issue here is authority.
When we position ourselves
in opposition to true authority,
we put ourselves in opposition to God.
This is the foundation of Satan's empire.
For many of us who come from the United States and Europe,
resistance and revolution are seen as virtues.

Many years ago,
my pastor,
Tommy Reid,
commented
that the Kingdom of God
is not a democracy.

There is only one King in the Kingdom.
In the Kingdom of God you don't lead a revolution.
That has been done before;
remember the devil?
In the Kingdom,
you come into alignment with the King.

In other words,
whose side are you on:
The King,
or the revolution against him?

This may bother you.
As I write this, I feel my own little soul rising up in rebellion.

One day, I was talking with my dear friend Bhari Long.
I told her how whenever God asks me to do something,
the Lord and I have a "discussion."
Bhari looked at me
and honestly said,
"Christ,
that's not a discussion,
that's
defiance."

                     She was right.

Stubbornness is like iniquity and idolatry.[46]
Derek Prince once said that
"stubbornness is making an idol of your own opinion."
How many times have you tried to talk with someone
and you discovered their mind was made up
and there was no changing them?
This is an idol.

We are back to the end of Judges,
and to the Sons of Eli.
Everyone does whatever is right in their own eyes.
Who are you to tell me what to do?
God loves me and I can do whatever I want.
Defiance.

The Bible puts Saul and David in sharp contrast
so that **we can see the values of the Kingdom of God.**
It is about where your heart is.
Saul was not a man after God's heart.

And in the end,
Saul consulted the witch of Endor,
and practiced divination
because God had stopped talking to him.
We all need supernatural help,
and if we can't get it from the good river,
we will go to the muddy cisterns.

We are fighting a supernatural war.
Satan is looking for allies, not victims.

You,
artist and creative person,
are called to be a warrior.

The solution to this big transition
that began with the Sons of Eli
ends with a worship revolution
and a promise to David that has not yet been fulfilled.
This promise involves you,
warrior artisan.

But before we get there,
we need a **heart adjustment.**
Are you willing to align your heart with the heart of God?
Are you willing to say "yes" to the authority of the Father?
Are you willing to say, like Mary,
"Let it be to me according to your word?"

> Father,
> I acknowledge
> that I have lived in a time
> when rebellion,
> resisting authority,
> and revolution
> are seen as virtues.
> And I acknowledge that the art world
> is defiant toward you and your Kingdom.
> Forgive me for every way
> I have resisted
> your authority,
> your word,
> and those you have put in authority.
> I know that when I resist them,
> I resist you.
> Soften my heart,
> and help me walk softly,
> listen to you,
> and hold all my rights and opinions
> lightly.
> I surrender and submit to you.
> Amen.

After God rejected Saul,
he looked for another after his own heart.
That one was David.

Becoming a Warrior

In a world of geopolitical powers
with industrial military complexes,
two worlds collide.

Zechariah saw this global military power.
His vision was of a war that encompassed the world.
He witnessed total war.

He saw the day that Jesus predicted in Matthew 24:
"And there will be wars,
and rumors of wars."

And in response,
God did not summon an equally powerful military force.
God summoned an elite group of warriors.

There is a difference between a warrior and a soldier.

A soldier is a cog in a large machine.
They function within an organization
where everything is rigidly dictated,
and where rank,
orders,
and control
are most important,
to make sure that commands are carried out,
and goals are achieved.

And the good soldier
takes orders and doesn't ask questions,
and lays aside his or her own
pain,
fear,
and
personal feelings
for the larger goals of the military power
who employs them.

They are part of the war machine.
A soldier is just a number on the roster.

A warrior is different.
A warrior is first motivated by their heart.
They are aligned with a cause.
They believe in what they are fighting for.
For a warrior,
the battle is personal.

Ideally,
a warrior is motivated
by a cause that is right.
And for most of history,
a warrior
fought for a king
and for their own land.
They fought with a personal investment.

In the Bible,
there is one person who exemplifies the warrior
more than any other.
David.

David was a shepherd.
David was a musician.
David was a dancer.
David was full of passions.
God says that David was a man after his own heart.[47]
And David was first,
and primarily,
a warrior.

Allan Tuffs, in his book,
And You Shall Teach Them to Your Sons,
describes a Jewish warrior this way:

> We must recognize the warrior spirit for what it is—that basic instinct in a man to defend what he loves. It is the impetus to fight for what he believes is right and just. It is the warrior spirit that moves a man to decisive action. It is that force within him that drives him to complete a mission despite daunting odds. The warrior spirit reveals itself in many ways. Bravery, duty, self-sacrifice, stamina, discipline, and skill are all expressions of the warrior spirit.[48]

This is the spirit that rose up in David
when he heard about the taunts made by Goliath
not just to the army of Israel,
but toward God.

It was this passion that rose up and caused him to respond.
"Your servant has killed
lions and bears
and this uncircumcised Philistine
shall be like one of them,
seeing he has defied the armies of the living God."[49]

**For the warrior,
a battle is personal.**

And it is in this moment,
that David,
the boy shepherd
and the court musician,
begins to emerge as a warrior.

There are several skills
that David developed
before he became a warrior.
There are some interesting parallels
with our study of the charashim.

David learned to live alone.
From the field of the shepherd,
David developed a relationship with God.
The relationship with God is forged in silence and solitude.

David learned the skills of keeping sheep.
He learned to handle a sling,
and developed the skills of a marksman.
He learned how to kill a lion and a bear,
and to fight
to protect the sheep
in his care.
In this experience,
he also developed a level of physical strength and stamina.

David developed his musical ability.
Somewhere out in the fields with the sheep,
he had learned to pass the time by making music
with a harp, and he began to compose lyrics.

And finally,
David was anointed.
Before David ever entered into battle,
he was anointed King,
and he received an impartation of the Holy Spirit.
And this final quality
would be the inner force that
enabled him to fight,
and to walk through many years
of **unfulfilled dreams, hopes, and promises**.

Unlike other kings,
David didn't fight to become king;
he fought to be seen as king.
His identity as king
was secure first.
He knew the end at the beginning,
and that made it possible to keep going.
A warrior doesn't fight from top-down orders.
The warrior fights from an inward promise.

All of these ingredients
contributed to the moment when
David emerges as a warrior,
and his first battle,
with Goliath,
is a tremendous victory.

So how do we become warriors?

Like we saw earlier,
the artisan warriors
are the ones who get quiet before the Lord.
You have to first narrow your focus.
You have to listen to one voice,
and perform for an audience of One.
An artisan warrior fights for one King.

Artisan warriors develop their skills.
These skills become like arrows in a quiver.

Ten years ago, I was having a conversation with
pastor Garris Elkins,
and he gave me some very wise counsel.
He said that all the things that have happened in my life
were like the ingredients in a slow cooker.
And up until midlife,
I didn't know what I was making,
but all of those skills and experiences
eventually would flavor the stew that I was creating.

For many years, I was not sure what I was doing:
going to seminary,
working as a professional musician,
artist,
writer,
and teacher.
A lot of it didn't make sense.
Now I am grateful for all those varied experiences,
because they are the foundation
for all that I do today.

Warriors
**take every situation and see it
as an opportunity to grow,
learn,
and develop.**

Warriors
are **focused.**
A warrior
only fights for the King and the Kingdom.

When I began my acting lessons,
the first skill that was emphasized
was **concentration.**
A good actor
gets into character,
and can concentrate
no matter what is happening around them.
This laser-like focus is an essential skill for the warrior.

Warriors,
after developing ability
and gaining focus,
**seek the Lord
and gain anointing.**

In all truth,
we are **fighting a supernatural war.**
And we have to fight a supernatural war
with supernatural weapons.

One afternoon,
I was watching a documentary
about the rise of the Nazi Party in Germany.
The program emphasized
the amount of time the Nazi leaders
engaged in occult activity
and called on the pagan Germanic gods of war for help.
They received supernatural help
to do the things they did.

And in that moment,
I asked God for the supernatural help
to do good for the Kingdom.
And the presence and power of the Holy Spirit
suddenly came over me.
Like David,
we cannot do this
without the power, person, and presence
of the Holy Spirit.

And finally,
warriors are disciplined.
As Will Durant said,
summarizing Aristotle,
"We are what we repeatedly do.
Excellence, then,
is not an act,
but a habit."[50]

Eugene Peterson put it this way:
"the Christian life is a long obedience
in the same direction."

David made it a habit to come into the presence of God,
just as he kept his body and his mind sharp.
It was not a one time act,
but rather a lifestyle over years.

At the same time,
David struggled.
He was a complex person.
And like many of the artists and creative people I know,
he experienced trauma.

Freedom from Trauma

When we look over the life of David,
there are several things that come to mind.

There are the promises,
and the poetry,
and the adventures.

Whenever a person has a big call from God,
there is going to be resistance and opposition.
David's life
can be summed up in one word
more than any other:
struggle.

We are first introduced to David
by his absence.
His father did not think David should
to be told that Samuel was visiting the family.

David himself wrote:
"Though my mother and father forsake me,
the Lord will always be at my side."[51]

Oddly, for a king,
there is little mention of his family,
other than his mother being "the handmaid,"
and his grandmother in the book of Ruth.
[52]

And in the Psalms, you see a lot of violent
emotional shifts,
from cursing to blessing in a matter of lines.
Dr. Mike Hutchings has pointed out that David
shows all the signs of trauma.
53

Here is the short list:
David was overlooked by his family.
As a boy, he killed lions and bears—
most likely because he had no other choice.
As a teenager, he killed and decapitated a man.
Around this time, he escaped being killed with a spear
by Saul multiple times.
As a young man, he had to flee as a fugitive
and live as refugee.
His best friend was killed at the hand of his own army.
He killed a man and tried to hide it.
His son led a civil war against him.
And at the end of his life, he had to intercept another coup
from a different son.

I sit with artists and creative people
and talk about their stories
a lot.

In the past eighteen years, I have dried a lot of tears
and heard a lot of unspeakable stories.

Struggling to get where God wants you
is part of the process of becoming a warrior artisan.
And a lot of folks give up
or sell out along the way.
The way
to fulfilling your calling is narrow.
There are many other broad ways to destruction.
To use a cliché:
the struggle is real.

All the stories I have listened to
have similar themes.
A lot of artists experience
rejection,

and some of this comes from
being misunderstood by family or peers.

Many, many people I meet have experienced
sexual,
physical,
or emotional abuse.

I have seen a lot of people
who have suffered financially
when churches and businesses either
took advantage of their gifts
and not paid them
or paid them less than agreed.

And then there is the pain that occurs
when a highly creative person is under-employed
or in the wrong job altogether, in order to pay the bills.

In fact, the long, slow
experience of neglect, financial insecurity,
homelessness, and lack of purpose
is far more damaging over time than any single event.

These patterns in our lives
can lock us into a mindset
that things are not going to change,
and the future lacks all possibilities.
We are back to that dull, gray city:
a metropolis of limitations.

In 2000,
I was diagnosed with Post Traumatic Stress Disorder.
For many years, I practiced coping mechanisms,
and worked hard to manage my life.
In my life,
Post-traumatic stress manifested
in violent, uncontrollable
emotional outbursts,
addictions,
a feeling that I had to be on guard all the time,
uncontrolled reactions to sounds, lights, and movement,

and patterns of crazy thoughts.
One counselor I met told me that I had control issues
that he could feel across the room.

The medical community describes trauma as a brain injury.
PTSD is a medical diagnosis,
and although there can be signs we recognize,
I am not a psychiatrist and I can't make this diagnosis.
From the time of my diagnosis,
I worked very hard to manage my problem.
Fortunately,
most of the time
I was able to cope through
regular rest,
deep breathing,
soaking prayer,
and diligent organization.
But they were just **coping mechanisms**
and the problem was always there.
And there were periods,
especially under ministry stress,
where I just could not control my actions.

When you work with Christians,
you soon discover that
no matter how good your long-term track record is,
if you have a bad day,
all is forgotten,
you are **marked as defective,**
and then you are removed.

As they say,
the church is the only army where people shoot
their own wounded.

Over the years,
I have discovered that trauma
is the **primary block to a person's creativity,**
and also one of the primary reasons
artists and creative people
withdraw and distance themselves from church.
It hurts too much.

And for full disclosure,
this isn't a scientific research paper.
I'm writing from my own life
and the anecdotal evidence that comes from
decades of working with hurting people.

In 2018,
a year after my dad's death,
a series of events triggered another
episode of PTSD.
I was completely unable to function,
and walked around under a cloud
of invasive thoughts,
heaviness,
and out of control emotions.
Those closest to me knew that something was deeply wrong,
and they began looking around for a way to help.

Trauma,
at its core,
is a landing strip
for the demonic in our lives.
It opens the door to oppression,
and at its root is a spiritual dynamic.
And this was obvious as I explored a series of
therapeutic solutions.
The most highly recommended therapies
involved some form of Eastern religious practice
or occult (in the guise of "New Age") activity.
I couldn't do that.

One day, a dear friend
told me about Dr. Mike Hutchings
and his team at Global Awakening
in Pennsylvania.
I was encouraged to go to a conference,
and a special appointment was set up for me to receive prayer.
Dr. Hutchings
had developed a way to pray for those
with post-traumatic stress
and he was seeing dramatic results.

I signed up to go.
As sometimes happens in New England,
we experienced
a terrible blizzard,
and all travel was stopped.

I was stuck at home
and decided to attend the conference online.

I learned a lot and took very detailed notes.
Two members from Dr. Hutchings' team
were going to be in Boston the next week,
so we arranged a time for me to receive prayer
after the event.

The information was good,
but it was also seriously triggering.
After the conference,
my symptoms became dramatically worse.
A few days after the conference,
I could take no more.
I took out my notes,
and I read them out loud.

And the crazy in my head stopped.

A few hours later,
another layer came up.
I did it again.
It stopped again.

The next day,
it happened again,
and it was a lot harder.
As I prayed,
I "saw" Jesus walk into the room
and help me while I prayed.
After the third time,
I was completely healed.

On the Saturday after,
I met the folks who were supposed to pray for me,

and we went out to dinner and had a lovely time.
No prayer session.

Since then,
I have prayed for many, many sufferers of
post-traumatic stress.

There have been a lot of miracles.
Yes, there have been physical healings,
but most significant
is watching men and women
who were locked up,
stuck,
and unable to create
experience freedom.
It is beautiful to see a person get their life back.

I want to share with you the simple process
that I use to pray for the effects of trauma.

**This is not magic,
and I encourage you to do this with someone else
rather than alone.**

This is a simple process,
and will be effective if you take your time
and listen to the leading of the Holy Spirit.

A Simple Model of Prayer for Trauma

Ask yourself, or the person you are praying for, these questions:
- Who hurt you?
- What happened?
- Pay attention to events of abuse, violence, war, neglect, abandonment, or pain.
- How did you respond to it?
- Do you feel anxious, hyper-vigilant, have trouble sleeping, or self-medicate?

Honor yourself or the other person.
- Let them know that it was never God's plan for them to suffer tragedy.
- Assure them that God has provided a way for healing and freedom.

Speak Isaiah 61:1-2:
"The Spirit of the Lord God is upon me, because the Lord has anointed me to bring good news to the poor; he has sent me to bind up the brokenhearted, to proclaim liberty to the captives, and the opening of the prison to those who are bound."

This is not a counseling session, but a healing prayer ministry session.
In this time, you are going to walk through a process of forgiveness, deliverance, and healing. If you have not made a commitment to Christ, you can experience some prayer, but the key parts of the healing will only come with faith in Jesus.

Forgive.
I walk everyone through a three step process of forgiveness.

- **Forgive others:** In the name of Jesus, I forgive _____ for hurting me.
- **Forgive yourself:** I forgive (say your own name) for any sinful reactions I may have to other people's sin. (If you have been involved in self-destructive behavior, it may be necessary to confess this sin.)
- **Release God:** God, I release you from any ways I hold you responsible for the pain in my life. I release you for not protecting me or preventing this trauma from happening.

Release the person.
Speak forgiveness over them.

I John 1:9: If we confess our sins, he is faithful and just to forgive us our sins and to cleanse us from all unrighteousness.

Romans 8:1-2: There is therefore now no condemnation for those who are in Christ Jesus. For the law of the Spirit of life has set you free in Christ Jesus from the law of sin and death.

Cancel and Cast Out.
Spiritual forces of darkness gain access through trauma.
It is important that the person receiving prayer keep eye contact with you, and that they just receive and respond, not pray or interrupt.

Listen to God and ask Him to show you any demons that need to be named and cast out. The Bible tells us, "if we resist the devil, he must flee." (James 4:7)
I have found that if I sense something reacting to the prayer, I breathe in and out and, if necessary, cough.
As you name things, **command them to leave the person and go to Jesus.**
When the Lord stops showing you things, **stop.** It's time to move on.
Ask the person to take a deep breath and breathe out one last time.
This should be simple and easy.
Usually, after this step, you will feel a lot of ease and lightness.

Pray for healing.
Speak 2 Corinthians 5:17 over the person.
"Therefore, if anyone is in Christ, he is a new creation. The old has passed away; behold, the new has come."

Place your hand over the heart and pray for the healing of the trauma. You may need to pray for a restoration of their sense of being, and a reconnecting of their head and their heart. Pray until you begin to see the person breathe naturally and deeply.

Place your hand on the right side of their brain. Imagine the neural pathways like little trees, speak to the pathways, and "cut them." Speak to every neural pathway related to trauma and declare that it must wither up and die. Speak to the new neural pathways to come forth. Bless the memory centers of the brain and speak to all the memories that have been blocked by trauma and call them forth. Speak to the natural sleep cycle to return to normal, and declare "that the Lord gives to his beloved sleep" (Psalm 127:2). Speak to the "pleasure centers" of the brain and declare that they will function normally. Cancel any patterns of addiction that the person has used to deal with pain.

Speak to the senses of sight, smell, taste, hearing, and touch, disconnect them from the trauma of the past, and declare that they will be only used to receive God's appointed messages and information. **Say, "The five senses will no longer be used as trigger points for trauma."**

Call the body and brain chemistry back into order, and bless the systems of the body.
I bless you,
Endocrine system.
Bones and teeth.
Muscles.
Circulation and Heart.
Lungs and respiration.
Digestion.
Reproduction.
Skin.

Have the person agree and respond:
I am a child of the King.
I am a co-heir with Jesus.
All Jesus bought and paid for is my inheritance.
I am loved.
I am forgiven.
I am cleansed by the blood.
I am accepted in the beloved.
I am filled with the Holy Spirit.
Jesus lives in me and transforms me from the inside out.
I have angels protecting me and assisting me in the ministry of Jesus.
I am united with Jesus.
I have been crucified with Christ.
I died with him. I was buried with him.
I have been raised with him.
I am seated with him in heavenly places,
above all rule and authority,
and above every name that is named,
not only in this age, but in the age to come.
I carry the authority of Christ.
I have authority over sickness,
over sin,
over demons,
and over the world.
I am the salt of the earth.
I am the light of the world.

All things work together for good in my life
because I love God,
and I am called according to his purpose.
I can do all things through Christ
because greater is He that is in me than he that is in the world.[54]

You may feel very tired in about an hour or so after the prayer, and so I encourage you to get some rest.

After the ministry session, pray the following prayer.

Lord Jesus, thank you for sharing with me your wonderful ministry of healing and deliverance. Thank you for the healings I have seen and experienced today. But I realize that the sickness and evil I encounter is more than our humanity can bear. So cleanse me of any sadness, negativity or despair that I may have picked up.

If my ministry has tempted me to anger, impatience or lust, cleanse me of those temptations and replace them with love, joy and peace. If any evil spirits have attached themselves to me or oppress me in any way, I command them to depart – now – and go straight to Jesus Christ, for Him to deal with as He will.
Come Holy Spirit, renew me, fill me anew with your power, your life and your joy. Strengthen me where I have felt weak and clothe me with your light. Fill me with life.

And Lord Jesus, please send your holy angels to minister to me and my family – and to guard us and protect us from all sickness, harm and accidents. (And guard us on a safe trip home.) We praise you now and forever, Father, Son and Holy Spirit![55]

After Healing Prayer

The following things can and do happen to people after a major healing or deliverance:
-
- Euphoria
- Exhaustion
- Change—some healings have a ripple effect, and many things change—
- relationships, situations, jobs.
- Relapse—sometimes things get worse before they get better.
- Mourning
- Celebration

How do you measure healing?

Keep a long-term perspective—I measure progress year to year,
not day to day.
Is there an "arc of improvement?"
Do things get better over time?
Is the person returning to the past?

How do you maintain healing?

Betty Tapscott put it best:

> God is the only one who can heal. He is the greatest psychiatrist, the greatest physician, the only healer. God will do his part, but each person must do his or her part also. Inner healing is a daily walk, a daily cleansing, a daily forgiving and being forgiven. It is not a "one-time experience," it is a process. We keep our inner healing by turning our backs on Satan, staying in God's word, praying, praising, staying in a Spirit-filled fellowship, and most importantly, keeping our eyes on Jesus.[56]

The most powerful thing you can do in the Kingdom
is to continue to walk out your healing.
The most powerful act of spiritual warfare
is getting healed and becoming a mature disciple of Jesus Christ.
You will probably need to go through this prayer
more than once.
Healing is a process of becoming.

Getting healed
is going to manifest in your life
and you will discover more and more
that your body is a weapon.

Your Body is the Weapon

A long time ago, it seems,
I was studying to be an actor.

Early on in theatre training,
one learns that
your primary "instrument"
is your body.
Theatre
is physical in nature.
Later on, I began voice training,
and again
my teacher said,
"Your body is the instrument.
Don't smoke,
don't drink booze,
and limit your coffee consumption.
All of these things will impact your voice."

My podcast audience
knows there is a raspy edge on my voice,
largely from too much coffee.

My friend,
Jim Leach,
recently said that
**our bodies are the primary technology
God uses to release the Kingdom of God
on the earth.**

When we look at David,
we are seeing a person who lived life to the full
in a human body.
Often when we talk about David,
the first image is the young man
with his sling,
running toward Goliath.

And then
generally,
many people think of the mature man,
nearly nude,
dancing with abandon
in his underwear
as the ark is brought into Jerusalem.

And again,
this man is also an adulterer,
and has many wives.
David's passion is expressed through his body as well.

I've never seen the real David by Michelangelo in Florence,
but I have seen a plaster cast of it in London.
Monumental doesn't quite capture it.
There is something about Michelangelo's David
that drives home the point:
this is a physical man
at home in his body.

And this body of David
is the one that was
prophetically anointed
king.

And out of his body would come the genetic line
of the Messiah,
the anointed one.

Jesus,
God in the flesh,
Incarnate,
fully lived in a physical body.

> You must not let sin reign in your mortal bodies or command your obedience to bodily passions, you must not let any part of your body turn into an unholy weapon fighting on the side of sin; you should, instead, offer yourselves to God, and consider yourselves dead men brought back to life; you should make every part of your body into a weapon fighting on the side of God; and then sin will no longer dominate your life, since you are living by grace and not by law.[57]

Many Christians separate their bodies
from their spiritual lives.
There is a deep disconnect between body, soul, and spirit.

If you are an artist
in the Kingdom,
your body is the point.
Your work
and your creative output
are all expressions
and extensions of your body.
And your body, as Paul said,
is the temple of the Holy Spirit.

**The human body is the only thing in creation
made to contain God.**

Later on in this book,
we are going to talk about rebuilding
the Tabernacle of David,
and the promise of building a throne in the earth
for Jesus.

But too often,
we hear things like this,
and we immediately think of programs
and organizations.
We think of structures
and we think of activities.
Most of this busy-ness
has little or nothing to do with what God wants to do in us.

Your body is the weapon.

And again and again,
we are asked to yield our bodies to the Holy Spirit.
Again and again,
we are called to offer our bodies to God
as our primary act of worship.

Think about this:
Jesus Christ
took on a physical body,
and fully embraced being human.
He yielded that body
to the torture of a cross,
and that body was pierced,
and his blood and water flowed.
And out of that
he birthed a new body:
the Body of Believers.

As he promised,
his body,
which he referred to as a temple,
was destroyed,
and on the third day,
he raised it up again.

And right now,
a man with a physical body
sits in heaven.

Being a human being is a good thing.
You were created to fully enjoy a relationship with God.
And you were created to enjoy that relationship
through a physical experience.

I know that some of you
may be thinking about sex.
And sex is part of it.
We are living in a sex-obsessed age,
not too far off from the grim world
imagined by Aldous Huxley
in Brave New World.

When we think about sex,
Christians quickly begin to think in negative terms.

Immorality is really
about direction.
You are created to worship
and be in connection with the Creator.
This creator is the Most Relational Being in the Universe.
And we are called daily to yield our bodies to God
as a spiritual act of worship.

Our issue isn't pleasure,
the issue is choosing a **higher pleasure.**
We are called to enjoy God,
be filled with the Holy Spirit,
and live out that joy in the Holy Spirit
everywhere we go.

It is out of our physical lives
that we bear spiritual fruit.
Love,
joy,
peace,
patience,
kindness,
goodness,
gentleness,
faithfulness,
and self-control
are not abstracts.
They are real things
that get lived out of our lives.

You are called to be a warrior artisan.
And that means not compartmentalizing
your physical experience
and your religious belief.
What you do with your body
is an expression of your relationship with
and focus on God.

When God created humanity,
he called humanity very good.
Becoming whole
and complete
means **embracing your humanness.**
It means that your thoughts and feelings
are real
and they need to be acknowledged and accepted.
It's okay to be you.
It's okay to be real.
It's okay to have problems.
It's okay to have successes.

When you become completely
pro-life
in this way
then you can embrace the fullness of
God's call.

You are the temple.
You are the tabernacle.
You are the carrier of the glory within,
and God promises that your body
will be surrounded with a fire around.

There is no disconnect.

God is not
interested
in buildings,
in programs,
or in projects.

**God is
interested
in human beings
who are whole,
complete,
and fully reflect his glory.**

Jesus did not die
for temples, buildings, or programs.

He died for the thing he made:
you.

We are going to keep coming back to worship.
Paul told us our spiritual act of worship was this:
to present your body as a living sacrifice.[58]

When you offer a sacrifice,
you are walking into
the fulfillment of God's promise
to create a kingdom of priests.

When we offer our bodies to God as worship,
we,
like the offerings in the Old Testament,
become holy.

Holiness is not the thing you do.
Holiness is not a tenet or belief.
Holiness is not ritual.
Holiness
is the thing you become
when your body becomes the offering of God.

And when you offer your body to God,
you become the wood for the fire
and you become the dwelling place of the Holy Spirit.
You become like Jesus
> who, though he was in the form of God,
> did not count equality with God a thing to be grasped,
> but emptied himself,
> taking the form of a servant,
> being born in the likeness of men.
> And being found in human form
> he humbled himself and became obedient unto death,
> even death on a cross.
> Therefore God has highly exalted him
> and bestowed on him the name which is above every name,
> that at the name of Jesus every knee should bow,
> in heaven and on earth and under the earth,
> and every tongue confess that Jesus Christ is Lord,
> to the glory of God the Father.[59]

This is not a one-time event,
or a theological construct that cannot be applied to reality.
God sees your human body as good,
and wants it to be an offering,
a place where his glory will dwell.
It is a daily lifestyle of submission and surrender.

Your body is made
to be full of the glory
and surrounded by fire.
And as an artist,
creative person,
performer,
content maker,
and thought leader,
God's glory and fire can attract and touch
every thing
your body and life
contacts and touches.

I often pray a prayer like this:

Father,
thank you that you made me.
With all my foibles and failures,
with all the things I don't like and don't accept,
I know you created something good.
I accept things as they are and
I present to you today
my body
as a living sacrifice.
I offer you my body as a temple of the Holy Spirit.
May I commune with you, Holy Spirit,
and live out the presence of God through this body.
I present it to you.
Use it as you will.
Speak to me
and help me walk in conscious contact with Jesus today.
Amen.

And it is out of that place that I can sit and receive
instruction from the Lord.

One of my favorite professors from Asbury,
Dr. Robert Tuttle,
once said that he was "charismatic"
because,
"I believe that the same power that was available
to Jesus and the apostles
is available to me today."

That power
is the power of the Holy Spirit in you.
As Paul tells us,
this is the mystery:
Christ in us,
the hope of glory.[60]

And that mystery of Jesus in us,
through the power of the Holy Spirit,
makes us people who can access the power of the next age.
We are supernaturally empowered to be warriors in this age,
for the age to come.

Have you started to see how this all fits together?
The battle that Zechariah envisioned
was a battle between two ages,
this age and the age to come.

And this battle is all about worship
and all about you living in this body
in this age
as if it was in the age to come.
And the first person to get a glimpse of this truth
was David.

A Worship Revolution

In 2007,
I was attending a leaders' training at the International House of Prayer
in Kansas City, Missouri.
I'm not sure who was speaking,
but they gave a long and detailed description
of David and a company of worshippers
in front of the ark.

I have two degrees in Bible and theology.
And I had no idea what they were talking about.
It was from I Chronicles,
and I had never read it.

One thing
I have learned over the years,
is that seminaries and Bible teachers
ignore the history and details
of the most important thing we do in church:
worship.

I just finished watching a long series of talks on church history
and the teacher made no mention of the biggest thing
in all the movements of God throughout history:
how people worshiped and how worship changes.

I know this,
because I was going to do my Ph.D. on the history of worship.
And my seminary,

a very fine one, if I must say,
completely ignored the most important thing
that happened in the five hundred year shift during the time of David.

The books of Samuel,
Kings, and Chronicles
outline a worship revolution,
and the price we pay when worship
gets corrupted.

And for us,
this is very important,
because a worship revolution
is going to be
an arts revolution.

Let's reconsider the Sons of Eli.
Remember them?
They did not believe God was holy,
and acted as such.
And because of them,
the ark was captured,
and taken to the Philistine temple;
and their god—
Dagon—
had a lot of problems as a result.

In the end Dagon was broken into pieces.

In that world,
the idol of a god was the god,
and so the Philistines were very upset
that their national god was being beat up
by the God of Israel.
And then, to make matters worse,
the people began to have tumors
and get infested with rats.

They decided to get rid of the ark and they put it on a cart.

Now remember,
there was no priesthood.

The ark has left Shiloh,
and everyone was doing whatever was right in their own eyes.
There is no going back to the way things were.
So the ark ends up in the care of a man named Eleazer
for twenty years,
and Israel mourns.
We have to believe
that this was as devastating
as the destruction of the temple was in later years.
The old wineskin is gone.

Sometimes we think there is safety in the old way.
And although it may give us comfort,
there is no going back once you pass
the point of no return.

Throughout all the five hundred year shifts
there is a shift and revolution in worship.
Just consider this:
the destruction of the temple in Israel
is a key event in three shifts in history.
First under the Sons of Eli,
then by the Babylonians in 586 B.C.,
and again by the Romans in 70 A.D.
A worship revolution is key to shifts in civilization.

All of these shifts throughout history take time.
In England, the Reformation
took almost one hundred and fifty years to work out.
And this shift
in Israel spanned the lifetimes of
Samuel, Saul, and David.
That's three generations.

David had to fight for his place.
Even though he was anointed king when he was a youth
he was thirty before he sat on the throne.

David was a warrior,
but he was also a worshiper.
And he had to fight for a place of worship.
As I mentioned before,

it was the anointing that kept David going
through the decades between his anointing as king,
and his sitting on the throne as king.

There is a lot of wisdom in this advice from the sage Jesus ben Sirach

> My son, if you come forward to serve the Lord,
>   prepare yourself for temptation.
> Set your heart right and be steadfast,
>   and do not be hasty in time of calamity.
> Cleave to him and do not depart,
>   that you may be honored at the end of your life.
> Accept whatever is brought upon you,
>   and in changes that humble you be patient.
> For gold is tested in the fire,
>   and acceptable men in the furnace of humiliation.
> Trust in him, and he will help you;
>   make your ways straight, and hope in him.[61]

Remember:
you and I are in a war.
God has given you promises,
and the most effective weapon the enemy has is **abortion.**
If the enemy can get you to give up and quit
before the promise comes to pass
then the empire of lies wins.
The most useful warriors
are the ones who have been tested and tried,
who have promises that take time to work out.

David had more promises than anyone else,
and he had to fight for them.

And eventually,
David took his place as king
and he rested from his enemies.

He was a man after God's own heart,
and his heart was for the ark.

Now remember,
Israel was still in transition from the days

when everyone did what was right in their own eyes.
David puts the ark on a cart,
and a man named Uzziah touches it
and he dies.

The ark is not just a box.
It is the **throne of God** on the earth.
And it is meant to be borne by four living creatures
just like the one it resembles in heaven.
David has an encounter with the fear of the Lord.
And David takes the ark
to the home of a gentile,
Obed Edom.

The fear of the Lord is key.
The Sons of Eli had no fear of God.
And the seed of a revolution in worship
is a holy fear of the Lord.

I often wonder why the ark went to Obed Edom.
Was it so that a gentile had to suffer
if something went wrong?
Scripture tells us nothing about Eleazar,
who cared for it for twenty years,
other than it was a time of shame.
In contrast,
Obed Edom,
the Edomite,
was **blessed.**

Blessing is the first motivation for this worship revolution.
David pays attention to the blessing.
And it was the desire for his nation
to be blessed that moved him
to get the ark
and bring it to Jerusalem.

And the revolution begins.

First,
He has Levites carry the ark
just like it was mandated in the Law.

And then David assembles all Israel at Jerusalem.

And in this act,
David reconvenes
the dispersed
and leaderless priesthood,
and the tribe of Levi that has been almost invisible for a generation.
And he prepares the ark to be brought up to Jerusalem.

And then the real worship revolution begins:

> David also commanded the chiefs of the Levites to appoint their brethren as the singers who should play loudly on musical instruments, on harps and lyres and cymbals, to raise sounds of joy. So the Levites appointed Heman the son of Joel; and of his brethren Asaph the son of Berechiah; and of the sons of Merari, their brethren, Ethan the son of Kushaiah; and with them their brethren of the second order, Zechariah, Ja-aziel, Shemiramoth, Jehiel, Unni, Eliab, Benaiah, Ma-aseiah, Mattithiah, Eliphelehu, and Mikneiah, and the gatekeepers Obed-edom and Je-iel.[62]

Note that Obed-edom is included among the names.

> So David and the elders of Israel, and the commanders of thousands, went to bring up the ark of the covenant of the Lord from the house of Obed-edom with rejoicing. [63]

> And because God helped the Levites who were carrying the ark of the covenant of the Lord, they sacrificed seven bulls and seven rams. David was clothed with a robe of fine linen, as also were all the Levites who were carrying the ark, and the singers, and Chenaniah the leader of the music of the singers; and David wore a linen ephod. So all Israel brought up the ark of the covenant of the Lord with shouting, to the sound of the horn, trumpets, and cymbals, and made loud music on harps and lyres.

And it says that David brought the ark
into a tent that David pitched for it.

And he appointed an army of Levites
to praise and exalt and thank the God of Israel
day and night, continually.

And in the midst of this,
he appointed Obed-Edom,
a gentile,
and **called him a Levite.**

David established a place of worship before the Lord,
a continual sacrifice of praise to God,
and this place was separate from Shiloh,
and the altar.

David established a tent of worship
before the ark.

How important was this worship revolution?
It produced the Psalms.
We are still
singing them
today.

A thousand years before the book of Acts,
David gathered
musicians
and dancers
before the ark
to worship God
almost face to face.
He included gentiles in this ministry
and it produced a body of material
that would become the songbook
for Jews and Christians forever.

We sometimes miss the details in the Bible.
David had two places of worship.
And out of this revolution,
David desired to create a permanent place
that would incorporate both into one:
a temple
where the sacrifices

and the ongoing singing and music
would be brought together.

It was all about worship.

It was a completely different kind of priesthood.

When God begins to shake things,
it is always about
getting rid of the old
and creating something new.
And the new
is a restoration and resurrection of pure worship.

This is one of the most important aspects of this
five hundred year shift.
It is a time of transformation.

> . . . about every five hundred years the empowered structures of institutionalized Christianity, whatever they may be at that time, become an intolerable carapace that must be shattered in order that renewal and new growth may occur.
>
> When that mighty upheaval happens, history shows us, there are always at least three consistent results or corollary events. First, a new, more vital form of Christianity does indeed emerge. Second, the organized expression of Christianity which up until then had been the dominant one is reconstituted into a more pure and less ossified expression of its former self.
>
> As a result of this usually energetic but rarely benign process, the Church actually ends up with two new creatures where once there had been only one. That is, in the course of birthing a brand-new expression of its faith and praxis, the Church also gains a grand refurbishment of the older one.
>
> The third result is of equal, if not greater, significance, though. That is, every time the incrustations of an overly established Christianity have been broken open, the faith has spread—and been spread—dramatically into new geographic and demographic areas, thereby increasing exponentially the range and

depth of Christianity's reach as a result of its time of unease
and distress. Thus, for example, the birth of Protestantism not
only established a new, powerful way of being Christian, but
it also forced Roman Catholicism to make changes in its own
structures and praxis.[64]

We are living in a time when all of this is happening.
The old is breaking, or being exposed.
Massive changes in worship are occurring,
and we don't know what the future holds.

The worship revolution
overseen by David
moved the heart of God,
and out of it birthed a promise.

David was given a throne in the earth.

The Throne of David

> The scepter shall not depart from Judah,
>   nor the ruler's staff from between his feet,
> until he comes to whom it belongs;
>   and to him shall be the obedience of the peoples.[65]

Psalm 132
gives us an emotional window
into what David experienced
as he prepared a place for God in the earth.

> Remember, O Lord, in David's favor,
>   all the hardships he endured;
> how he swore to the Lord
>   and vowed to the Mighty One of Jacob,
> "I will not enter my house
>   or get into my bed;
> I will not give sleep to my eyes
>   or slumber to my eyelids,
> until I find a place for the Lord,
>   a dwelling place for the Mighty One of Jacob."[66]

Indeed David
did endure hardships.
First, he had a family that overlooked him.
Then he was anointed King
and was given a place in the court of Saul.
Saul turned on him

and pursued him for years.
This forced David to live as an outlaw and a fugitive.

**Whenever you have a creative call from God,
you are going to have to walk through many tests and trials
before you see the promise fulfilled.**
Perseverance,
tenacity,
and the ability to not give up
are incredible weapons for the Kingdom of God.

And after all this,
we have seen that David initiated a worship revolution.
David was a singer,
and a poet.
David was a dancer.
And David was a prophet.
We often forget
that David was also a dreamer
and a planner.
And from what we can tell,
David was a designer.

Many leaders have what I call
dream projects.
Many scholars
have a topic that they come back to and explore
in their free time.
Personally,
I have had seasons where I dipped into film study.
And someday, I am going to write a commentary on
John and Revelation from the point of view of an artist.
It's a dream project.
And David was no different.

In the midst of wars,
family squabbles,
and personal failures,
David dreamed of a temple for God.
He wanted to
incorporate this
new worship revolution

in Jerusalem
with the broken-down sacrificial system
that was mandated by God.
He wanted a place for God
that was a palace.
**It was the marriage of the plan of God,
and the plan of a man.**

The Temple was never God's plan.
And honestly,
I don't think the plan was ever to have a Tabernacle in one place.
I think it was intended to roam
throughout the earth,
as God's Kingdom advanced.
Israel never understood this.

David
was a renaissance man.
He was a polymath.
He was extremely creative.
And the Bible tells us
that he began to plan for the building of a Temple for God.
He consulted Nathan the Prophet about his plans.
Although Nathan agreed with David,
God had other thoughts:

> "Go and tell my servant David,
> 'Thus says the Lord:
> You shall not build me a house to dwell in.
> For I have not dwelt in a house since the day I led up Israel to this day, but I have gone from tent to tent and from dwelling to dwelling.
> In all places where I have moved with all Israel, did I speak a word with any of the judges of Israel, whom I commanded to shepherd my people, saying, "Why have you not built me a house of cedar?"'
>
> Now therefore thus shall you say to my servant David, 'Thus says the Lord of hosts, I took you from the pasture, from following the sheep, that you should be prince over my people Israel; and I have been with you wherever you went, and have cut off all your enemies from before you; and I will make for

you a name, like the name of the great ones of the earth. And I will appoint a place for my people Israel, and will plant them, that they may dwell in their own place, and be disturbed no more; and violent men shall waste them no more, as formerly from the time that I appointed judges over my people Israel; and I will subdue all your enemies.

Moreover I declare to you that the Lord will build you a house. When your days are fulfilled to go to be with your fathers, I will raise up your offspring after you, one of your own sons, and I will establish his kingdom. He shall build a house for me, and I will establish his throne for ever. I will be his father, and he shall be my son; I will not take my steadfast love from him, as I took it from him who was before you, but I will confirm him in my house and in my kingdom for ever and his throne shall be established for ever."[67]

**David's desire
was not the plan of God,
but David's desire moved the heart of God.**

Many artists come to me afraid of missing God's will for their lives.
If you are walking with God
in a good relationship,
God trusts you.
If you trust in the Lord,
**God will give you good desires,
and God will bless those desires.**

David was a man
who did not see God as someone to fear,
or someone who needed to be served
and pleased.
David knew God as a friend
and wanted a place for God in the earth.
It is all about relationship
and all about worship.
And because David
thought about God **first**,
the Lord responded.

In essence,
God said,
"David,
your kingdom
is now going to become my Kingdom."
**God took the name David
and made it his own.**

A thousand years later,
another son of David appeared,
and he began preaching a kingdom.

Jesus came to establish the Kingdom of God,
but he also came to establish the Kingdom of David.

> The Lord swore to David a sure oath
>   from which he will not turn back:
> "One of the sons of your body
>   I will set on your throne.
> If your sons keep my covenant
>   and my testimonies which I shall teach them,
> their sons also for ever
>   shall sit upon your throne."[68]

The writers of the New Testament understood this,
and it is clear
the apostles also knew it.
When the decision to allow gentiles into the church was made,
they pointed to Amos 9:11-12:

> "In that day I will raise up
>   the booth of David that is fallen
> and repair its breaches,
>   and raise up its ruins,
>   and rebuild it as in the days of old;
> that they may possess the remnant of Edom
>   and all the nations who are called by my name,"
>   says the Lord who does this.

The worship revolution
under David—
the tent for the Ark of the Presence

presided over by a gentile—
was the prophetic sign of the
New Covenant in Jesus.

It is all about worship.
It is all about relationship.
It is all about the Kingdom.
**And a worship revolution
is a revolution in the arts.**

Our God is the Most Relational Being in the Universe,
and this relationship with David
was so significant to God,
**that he chose David
to be the genetic material
for his Incarnation.**

> Yes, you can say wow.

And because of this,
the promises to David and his descendants
are shared by us.

This God is really good.

This book is about artists at a time of war.
And this is where the threads I have been showing you
begin to come together.
**God is calling us to be elite warriors in a world
committed to bringing us despair.**

The army of warrior artists is fighting
not with weapons,
but with ideas,
thoughts,
images,
pictures,
sounds,
and worship.
And our army
is fighting
to establish a kingdom.

**And that Kingdom
is the Kingdom of God,
and also the Kingdom of David.**

You see,
Jesus is coming back.
And when he comes back,
he is going to sit on a throne.
And that throne
is the throne of David.
It will be from the seat of David
that Jesus rules and reigns on the earth.
And it will be the fallen tent of David,
the tent of the Presence,
the tent of Jew and gentile together,
in constant praise and thanksgiving
where this throne sits.

The book of Isaiah
ends with many of the themes we have touched on so far.

> Thus says the Lord:
> "Heaven is my throne
>   and the earth is my footstool;
> **what is the house which you would build for me,
>   and what is the place of my rest?**
>
> All these things my hand has made,
>   and so all these things are mine,
>   says the Lord.
> But this is the man to whom I will look,
>   **he that is humble and contrite in spirit,
>   and trembles at my word.**[69]
>
> For thus says the Lord:
> "Behold, I will **extend prosperity** to her like a river,
>   and the wealth of the nations like an overflowing stream;
> and you shall suck, you shall be carried upon her hip,
>   and dandled upon her knees.

> As one whom his mother comforts,
>   so I will comfort you;
>   you shall be comforted in Jerusalem.[70]
>
> "For I know their works and their thoughts, and I am coming to gather all nations and tongues; and they shall come and shall see my glory, and I will set a sign among them. And from them I will send survivors to the nations, to Tarshish, Put, and Lud, who draw the bow, to Tubal and Javan, to the coastlands afar off, that have not heard my fame or seen my glory; and they shall **declare my glory among the nations.** And they shall bring all your brethren from all the nations as an offering to the Lord, upon horses, and in chariots, and in litters, and upon mules, and upon dromedaries, to my holy mountain Jerusalem, says the Lord, just as the Israelites bring their cereal offering in a clean vessel to the house of the Lord. And some of **them also I will take for priests and for Levites, says the Lord.**
>
> "For as the new heavens and the new earth
>   which I will make
> shall remain before me, says the Lord;
>   **so shall your descendants and your name remain.**
> From new moon to new moon,
>   and from sabbath to sabbath,
> **all flesh shall come to worship before me,**
>   says the Lord.[71]

God's plan is prosperity.
God's plan is all nations.
And God's plan is worship.
And out of the nations,
God will make Levites.

And his Kingdom will have no end.

**The artist at the end of time
will be a little bit charashim
and a little bit David.**

The glory of God will be in you,
and the presence of God will be all around you.

And out of your abundance,
the wealth of nations will flow.
Wealth is not just cash.
Wealth is the resources of heaven.
Wealth is the ability to create new solutions
for old problems.

Wealth is the ability to see what is possible.
And it is a way forward
in the midst of
the wreckage of war
and the fog of despair.

We are living in an already,
but not yet,
kingdom.

In the next section,
we are going to come to something I said a few chapters ago.
In a time of
war,
change,
and transition,
we can either be victims of circumstance
or we can overcome.

Daniel and his companions
overcame in the camp of the enemy,
Babylon.

Part III

DANIEL IN BABYLON

By the Waters of Babylon

Five hundred years after David,
the worship revolution has long been forgotten.
Solomon introduced a multitude of foreign gods into Israel,
after he completed his father's dream of a house for God.

Finally,
the temple was destroyed in 586 BC,
and most of the people were carted off to Babylon.

Again,
a point of no return happened.
The temple was no more.
And the best and brightest found themselves in the court of Babylon.

All of these five hundred year shifts
have an interesting
thing in common.

How people worship God
goes through a shift,
and one of the shifts common to many of them
involves language.
This certainly is the case in the period after Vatican II.

After the Jews go to Babylon,
their language
undergoes a transformation
from proto-Hebrew

to what we would recognize as Biblical Hebrew.
And it is during this time
that various oral traditions
collected scrolls,
and stories
get collated into what we would recognize
as the core of the Old Testament.

Two thousand years later,
another shift would occur
and the Bible would again undergo a language change,
and various translations,
including the King James Bible,
would emerge.

These shifts are connected to the Word.
The shaking produces very important fruit,
where the Bible reaches a larger audience.

From the exiles to Babylon,
the King requested that the brightest and best
be brought into the court,
and among these was a group of young men:
Daniel, Hananiah, Mishael, and Azariah.

The Babylonians took away their Hebrew names
and gave them pagan ones;
Daniel was called Belteshazzar,
and the other three,
you probably know,
were called
Shadrach,
Meshach,
and Abednego.
And we can see very clearly here,
that Babylon is not safe,
and Babylon is not home.
And yet,
by the waters of Babylon
where others sat and wept,
Daniel learned to succeed and thrive.

The first key to thriving by the waters of Babylon
is that Daniel knew who he was.
Although
they gave him a new name,
inside
he was always Daniel.
And he knew
that he would not bow down to any other god
than the God of Israel.
This was his starting point.
Daniel was certain of his identity.
And so,
when he was asked to eat the rich food from the table of the King,
he needed wisdom.

Working **within** the structures
of the court,
Daniel went to the chief steward
and asked if he could eat only vegetables.

And humbly,
Daniel took full responsibility for his decision,
and said that if he was not as healthy,
or suffered for this choice,
he would suffer whatever consequences.

After a while,
it became clear:
Daniel was healthier and more clear headed
than the others in the court.
Babylon is not home.
The **mistake** made by many Christians in the arts
is the belief that Babylon is home
and that you need to **cooperate with Babylon**
in order to make a difference.

Daniel
understood
that Jerusalem was home
and that this place where he found himself
was not and never would be home.

There was a **system** here,
but he could not submit to it.

Ironically,
the Christian music business is far more
business than the stuff I encountered in the "secular" world.

I worked for a long time in a "liberal" denomination.
More than once, I found myself in tricky situations.
I learned
(the hard way)
that one needs to choose one's battles carefully.
If you know who you are,
you don't have to argue or make your point.
I have made a lot of
unusual
friends and allies
over the years
because I chose not to fight
over things that were not important.
**Just because it may be important to them
doesn't mean it has to be important to you.**

Sometimes,
when asked a difficult question,
I learned that it was better to say
"Oh, that's interesting."
Rather than to voice my disgust.
And other times,
when you are asked to violate your conscience,
you say **no.**

There is always a price to pay for saying no,
but often
people **respect** you
for being solid
and having principles.

Nobody respects a sellout.
They say that everyone has a price.
If you know who you are on the inside,
then you won't be tempted to sell out.

You will stand for who you are,
from the inside out.
Priceless.

Many of us
who work in the arts
get asked to submit to Babylon.
When this happens, **you have several options.**

The majority of Christians **retreat** into a bubble,
and try to avoid the world system.
The result is second-rate art that doesn't get critiqued or challenged
and a world that suffers with no salt and light.
That's why Christian art is often bad:
It doesn't have to meet the professional standard.

Some try to stay in the system
but **compromise** to get ahead,
thinking that will help them get influence in the future.
Unfortunately,
compromise often leads to corruption.
Often, these become the high profile celebrities
who publicly lose their faith.

One morning I was praying in the Massachusetts State House
when a woman carrying a box of coffee and donuts
asked me to open the door for her.
Within moments,
I found myself in the office of the most corrupt
politician in Massachusetts,
and I was engaging in conversation
with her assistant!

We had an interesting chat,
and she was intrigued that I was praying,
but I didn't have a political agenda.
As we ended our conversation,
she thanked me.

And as I left,
I realized,
no one sets out to be a crooked politician.

It starts with a little compromise
here and there,
with good intentions.
And eventually,
you soon realize that you are part of the system
and part of the problem,
not part of the solution.
This is why Jesus said to **judge a tree by its fruit**,[72]
not by its good intentions.

The third option
for the Christian in the arts
is like Daniel in Babylon.

You face the situation.
You don't run from the challenge
but into it,
and you begin,
from your inner knowledge of who you are,
to make clear decisions.
Daniel didn't have a choice with his circumstances.
We do.
We don't have to go to a school that will set out to undermine us.
We can choose where we audition, or where we apply.
But even then, we have to be firm against
the **prevailing culture** of Babylon.

You have to settle it before the test.
"I will not eat from the table of the king
because I keep kosher."
Daniel and his companions
made a choice.
They did it respectfully,
but also honorably.
And that little choice
in a not so difficult situation
made it easier to make other choices.

I won't bow down to the idol you have made.
I won't worship the king as a god.

And in every case,
Daniel was raised up higher,
with more respect
and honor.

We are not living in a Judeo-Christian culture for the moment.
Things are in flux.
We are living in Babylon.
You can sit and weep
and wish for the way things were,
you can protest and have a fit,
or you can face facts.

**Babylon is dangerous,
and Babylon is not your home.**

And you need to know who you are.
You were made in the image of God.
You were bought by the blood of Jesus Christ.
You were called out of darkness into his marvelous light.
You are called to be light in the dark,
and salt in a world that is without flavor.
You are filled with the Holy Spirit,
and your body is his temple.
You are living for another age,
and you are commissioned to release that age
into this one.
You are called to believe on the Lord Jesus Christ
and love other people,
all the time.

If you know these things,
and things are clear in your heart and mind,
then you can choose rightly and wisely.
You don't have to retreat.

The next thing that is really important
is to have a Kingdom grid
and a Kingdom perspective.

The Kingdom Grid

Since 2005,
I have placed a high value on listening to God
and being open
when someone comes to me
and wants to share a word from God for me.

Many things in the Christian life
are meant to be held in tension.
I am open and receptive,
and I am also careful and discerning.
I hold all the words
I receive from people **loosely**,
and **test** everything against the Bible
and the long history I have with Jesus.

Many people settle for a low-level prophetic flurry
and are always running after the next "word."
And because of this,
they miss what God is really saying
in the pursuit of **religious entertainment.**

One day, two women came into the house of prayer
I was leading in Akron, Ohio.
They spoke to me about God moving me to my next assignment,
and that I was going to go with nothing but a suitcase,
and when I arrived at my next location,
I would be like Daniel:
I would teach the people "a new way to eat."

At the time,
I responded by saying
"I don't receive that."
The women were gracious.
They came back two weeks later
and repeated the word verbatim.
And now, almost twenty years later,
everything they said has come to pass.

Daniel,
five hundred years after David,
was taken into captivity to Babylon.
Rather than eat a diet that was not Kosher,
he chose to eat only vegetables.
His example forced all the others in the court around him
to eat like he did.

This cryptic phrase,
"a new way to eat,"
seemed like a mystery for many years,
until I faced the problem
that I mentioned earlier in this book.

God is calling artists and creative people
to lead
in this new beginning
of another era in history.
And right now, there is a war over
what direction history will take.

But,
many artists and creative people
are weighed down with theology
and teaching that
misrepresents what the Bible
has to say about art and artists.
They are **saddled with a history** of iconoclasm
in the protestant church,
and with a **deep-seated insecurity**
about being an artist
that has its roots in the Enlightenment.
I still regularly talk to young people

fresh out of art school
who struggle with the need
to go get a
"real job."

I have already talked about my commitment to not apologize.
For much of the past ten years,
I have devoted my daily study to
Biblical roots in Hebrew,
Greek exegesis,
and the development of ideas
as they relate to artists.

This is all about teaching you,
gentle reader,
a new way to eat.

Rather than the artist being the foreman
in the factory of idols,
the artist
in Scripture,
is **painted as the clearest representation** of
the image of the Father,
who is described as the
"Author of Beauty"
in the intertestamental book of Wisdom.[73]

In early 2020,
I found myself in a predicament.
The entire world was locked down
and I was stuck in a bedsit apartment
at the top of Portobello Road
in London.

Two interesting things happened.
Because our community is dispersed,
we moved our regular prayer meetings
to video conferencing in 2018.
So when the pandemic hit,
we had already used video conferencing for two years.
**Our established online community
eventually birthed a virtual church.**

We called it Beth Charashim: the House of Artisans.
It still meets weekly online,
and now has a dedicated invisible podcast congregation that also listens weekly.
Our "seen and unseen" community is around one hundred artists.

We also birthed a daily prayer meeting.
Taking a cue from Jackie Pullinger's book,
Chasing the Dragon,
we pray together in tongues
for the global army of artists
every weekday for fifteen minutes.

So the first thing that came out of the lockdown
was a **whole new expression** of community.

The second thing
was much more dramatic.
I decided, since I had time,
to read my daily Bible readings in **Greek**.

It did not take long
before I saw a lot of problems in the Bible I was using.
I discovered my English Bible
was like reading the original through a distorted lens.
And it became more and more obvious to me
that this lens was related to the problems I faced
in writing to my audience:
artists and creative people.

And then there was this
nagging
little
problem
in my head.

**What about those places in the Bible
where you read something
and it just doesn't make sense
or it doesn't fit?**
What I was learning about the original language
and the arts

had a bigger implication:
**what if there were other places where the words
or ideas were distorted
to fit a grid?**

Now this doesn't mean the translators
were being deceptive.
It means they operated out of a grid.
I learned this when
I was working on my two books on Bezalel.

Because most Bible scholars
come from the Reformed tradition,
they are **predisposed to "unsee" the arts.**
They are also often extremely
left-brained,
rational thinkers.

They **overlook and undervalue artistic language**
because of their larger grid.

And the Bible translation reflects this.
An example of this is
the *New American Standard Version*
translation of the Psalms:
it is a book of poetry
with absolutely no poetic language or sensitivity.

And many versions
translate the artistic words in Exodus 35
in the **least** artistic way possible.
To this end, I heard a well-known ministry call
Bezalel the "greatest church administrator in history."

This is a reflection of a grid,
and it is so deeply engrained that those who use it
would be hard pressed
to recognize it.

And when I have sat down to talk with a Bible scholar,
the conversation sometimes becomes pretty heated.
The speck in their eye

is the way they see.
And all they see is the plank in mine.

This is why our grid is important.
Some people call them worldviews,
or perspectives,
or points of view.
But grids are the filters **everyone uses**
as a short cut way to process information.
And for many people,
their theological grid
is far **more important** than the information they are processing.

Theology is a system used to organize a grid.
For some, these systems
are more important
than the Bible itself,
and the real experiences people have with God.
This is why there are dozens of websites
dedicated to saying healings do not happen
and lives do not change
because it doesn't agree with the Reformed grid.
The grid is most important.

**Recognizing your grid
requires humility,
and the desire to see the truth.**

All of these ideas
came together
when I was sitting in my room in London,
reading Greek
and thinking about my inaccurate Bible,
and the army of artists I was called to raise.

I came up with a crazy idea.

Why don't I lay aside the grid
that I learned in seminary
and try out a new one?

Since this was an experiment,
and it might take a few trials and errors,
I thought I would just try one
and see what happened.

I started with the beginning of Mark's gospel.
Jesus came out of the wilderness
and he came preaching one message:

"Transform your thinking, for the Kingdom of Heaven is at hand."[74]

So I decided
I would start with the Kingdom of God.
Maybe the whole Bible is about the Kingdom?
And anytime I came upon a place in the Bible
that did not make sense,
or I normally skipped over,
I would ask myself this little question:

What does this have to do with the Kingdom of God?

Two things became clear right away:
first,
most of the arguments
and discussions
Christians get embroiled in
have nothing to do with the Kingdom,
but rather,
with their grids colliding.

When grids collide,
you have a lot of religious controversies.
And this conflict is not new.
Most of the problems
that people had with Jesus in the New Testament
were about religious issues.

And second,
I discovered that the Kingdom grid worked.

I have now taught the Bible
for over three years

in an attempt to understand the Bible
through a Kingdom filter.
This filter has helped us as a community
understand passages of scripture
that seemed to be shrouded in mystery.
A lot of things make more sense than they did before.

Getting a Kingdom grid
has also taken my teaching out of the realm of the abstract:
from a set of "correct beliefs"
that have no relationship to reality
to a practical life
where we are seeing real fruit in the lives of people.
As Jesus said,
the lame walk,
the blind see,
the deaf hear,
the poor hear the good news.

There is **no disconnect** between the Kingdom of Jesus,
what we believe,
and how it works out in our lives.

If we are living in enemy territory,
and surrounded by danger,
we need things that work,
not unquestioned answers to
questions no one really asks anymore.
We need a solid foundation
rooted deeply in the life and teachings
of our Lord and Master.
He was giving us a Kingdom grid.

So what are the basic ideas behind this grid?

The Father is the Most Relational Being in the Universe.
The goal of the Christian life is for you to sit down at the Father's table and eat with him.
It is all about relationship.

We were created to be fulfilled in relationship
with the Father and with one another.
In the New Covenant, there is only one law: love one another.
Again, it is all about relationship with one another and with God.
This is why forgiveness is so important.

God chose a people, Israel,
to be a Kingdom of Priests in the earth,
but they have not walked into their calling.
Out of Israel, God raised up a son, Jesus Christ,
and he is the King of the Kingdom.
One of the things that is helpful in understanding the Kingdom grid is
understanding Hebrew as opposed to Greek ways of understanding the New Testament.
We have tried to humbly understand the Jewish ideas and ways of thinking in the Bible.
Most important is the concept that truth is often two ideas held in tension
rather than a set of precepts that form arguments.

The Kingdom of God began with the preaching of Jesus.
Jesus initiated the Kingdom with his preaching, and with his life.
Jesus displayed that those who were in the Kingdom
would do the same things he did, and also greater things.

The Legal Foundation of this Kingdom is the New Covenant in Jesus' Blood:
the eating of bread and the drinking of wine as a sign of the mystery of the faith:
Christ has died, Christ is risen, and Christ will come again.
Both the New Testament
and the witness of the early church
speak of the "breaking of the bread"
as the central act of Kingdom worship.
If you want to know more, read my book, *Body: Where You Belong*.

We come into the Kingdom through baptism and are given the Holy Spirit.
This is the witness of the book of Acts,
and baptism and the Holy Spirit cannot be separated.

Through the Holy Spirit, we experience the life of Jesus in us,
and we get a foretaste of the future full Kingdom age.
First and foremost, the Holy Spirit is the Presence, Power, and Person of Jesus in us.

The Holy Spirit empowers us with gifts and graces to live in two ages—
this one that is ending, and the new one that is beginning.
The Kingdom is essential and intrinsically charismatic.
The Holy Spirit is the organic life force in all that we do and believe.

Jesus is going to return to rule and reign on the earth
and fulfill all the promises God made to Israel
and the full human family who has entered the Kingdom.
Babylon is going to end.

Until that happens,
we are called to be living copies of Jesus,
the Icon of the Father.
This is why we are disciples.
We are being shaped and transformed into the image of the Father.

We do this by learning to listen to God and by doing what he tells us.
This book was the product of this revolution in my thinking.

There is a lot here that we don't have space or time to unpack.
I highly recommend reading *Very God: An Artist Looks at the Nicene Creed*.

In order to understand
the role of the artist during this five hundred year shift,
we have to understand our place in the Kingdom.

When you talk about being a "Christian" artist,
you immediately bring up a lot of **religious baggage**.

Are you an iconographer in the Orthodox sense?

Can you even do this if you are Presbyterian?

If you are a Baptist,
does that mean you have to put Bible verses in the work,
stop and preach,
and make sure everyone gets an opportunity to say
the "sinner's prayer?"

These are the kinds of questions
that I get asked quite often.
The religious grid is pretty big.

On the other hand,
**an artist in the Kingdom
is a normal person,
full of the Holy Spirit,
and gifted and graced
to expand and live in the Kingdom.
You can do this full-time
wherever you are as a person.**

It is for freedom that Christ has set you free.[75]

And this reality,
to many religious people,
sounds terrifying.
How do you **control** free people?

Fortunately,
there are some really simple and profound ways
to walk out a Kingdom lifestyle
like Daniel did.
You can thrive by the waters of Babylon
and overcome in a world that is shifting.

The Ancient Pathways

As I said earlier,
we are in a **collective identity crisis.**
For many of us,
we feel like the world around us
has lost its way.

We are back to the wilderness
and the road
and a sudden twist
that has led us into the middle of Babylon.

The word "icon"
appears roughly twenty-three times in the New Testament.
In many places it does not get translated accurately.

One of the most important places
where this word appears
is in Colossians 1:15.

**Christ is the visible icon,
the perfect portrait of the Father.**

As Jesus said,
if you have seen me,
you have seen the Father.[76]

So identity is not just being aware of who you are.
Identity is part of your inner make up.

Jesus was intrinsically
an icon of the Father.

Because we are in Christ
in the Kingdom,
full of the Holy Spirit,
we are Incarnated
and designed to be like Jesus.
We are called to be Master Copies
of the Icon of the Father.

This is what the word "discipleship" meant in the ancient world.

At the time of Jesus,
it was expected that a philosopher would grow a group of followers.
They would eventually learn
to talk like him,
look like him,
and act like him.

We want to
learn from Jesus,
talk like Jesus,
and act like Jesus.

In the 1990s, I was in a training session with Richard Foster.
He had created a program called Renovaré,
and I was a big fan.
I will never forget him
talking about going to many different church leaders
about the need for discipleship.

He said there was no church that had a plan for making disciples.
I thought about that a lot over the years.
I work with artists and creative people.
I have learned that any discipleship model
has to be simple,
adaptable,
and **not put pressure on you to conform to something.**

If you are going to overcome in Babylon,
you have to become a disciple.
You have to become a living copy
of the Icon of the Father.
The core principles of how you do this
are in the book of Daniel.

Essentially,
it boils down to this:
**Listen to the Lord,
and do what He tells you.**

In order to listen,
you need to do a few things.
Quiet yourself.
Learn how God speaks in the Bible,
and learn how to stay in contact with God
throughout the day.

In order to do what God says,
you have to learn to quiet yourself in every situation,
and you need to learn how to draw on the
supernatural help of God.
You cannot do it alone.

This is the ancient path.
What is interesting about this ancient path
is that it never gets old.
Even if
you keep repeating the same rhythms and patterns,
you are still engaging with a
living,
eternal,
ever-increasing
Person.
The Ancient Path is always alive and
always fresh.

When you learn to walk the Ancient Path
you soon discover that listening to God
also helps you discover your true identity.
The longer you do this,

the more "real" you become.
And this, too,
keeps the rhythm fresh.
And if it isn't,
that means there is an interruption in the flow.
This can simply be fixed,
usually through
forgiveness,
and letting go of anger.
These are the things that stop the life of God flowing in our lives.

Fairly often,
someone comes to me
and asks me to show them how to listen to God.

I tell them it is very simple.
You need to get a fresh notebook,
a pen or pencil,
and you need to read the daily gospel reading.[77]

I ask people to start from a fresh place.
A new notebook
is important
because **this is not journaling**.
We are not looking for a record of our own thoughts and feelings.
We are looking to get a record of what
we think
God is saying to us.

The reason I say
"we think"
is that no one hears the Voice of God
accurately all the time.
We need to keep a record
so that we can start to find out
what is the Voice of God
and what is the voice of our flesh
and sometimes,
what might be the voice of the devil.
So we keep a record,
and **we ask someone else** to go over it with us.

Usually, folks are shocked that
the first thing God says to them is
how much He loves them,
how valuable they are,
and how big his plans are for them.

This seems to happen to everyone.

The reason I ask people
to read the daily gospel reading
is so they can become tuned to the voice of Jesus.
Many people have spent too much time reading Paul,
or their pet passages of scripture,
and not Jesus.
We need to learn from Jesus.
He is the rabbi;
he is the Icon of the Father.
We need to get a sense of how Jesus sounds
and how Jesus would behave.
And this opens up a pathway in our soul
to be more tuned to the voice of the Shepherd.

The Kingdom pathway
is an ancient one.
This is the path that Abraham walked.
It is the path David walked.
And it is the path you must walk if you want to make it through
your sojourn in Babylon.

So the listening to God part is important,
but **so is the doing part**.
For some Christians,
they think God wants them to perform for him.
Sometimes, God will give you an assignment or a direction,
but in the initial phase,
you are really learning about who God is,
and who you are.

When the Lord does start to ask you to do things,
sometimes they will be mundane and simple.
Sometimes they will be uncomfortable,

like: go call someone you have hurt.
And then sometimes,
God will ask you to do big things.
And almost all the time,
the thing God asks you to do
will require obedience,
and his help.

That's the point.
**You never develop or mature
to the point of independence.**
If anything,
you become more and more
dependent on the Lord
all the time.

This ancient pathway
is key to overcoming in Babylon,
but it is also key to becoming a warrior artisan.

A warrior fights for a king,
remember?

And, fortunately,
we can take orders directly from the King.
And hopefully,
as you grow and mature,
you will start to see that this doesn't lead to confusion.
This leads to harmony and order
with **others who are also listening to God.**
And you will start to see the beautiful
poetry of the Father.

Now of course,
there are immature people
who hear things
and think that God told them things to do.
And they use this as permission to justify
making trouble for churches,
leaders,
and communities.

This is why tuning yourself to Jesus
and having someone else review what God is showing you
is so important.

**If you think God is telling you something
that you can't imagine Jesus saying or doing,
then stop right now.**

Jesus didn't overturn the market in the temple all the time.
And if your pastor is not openly preaching false doctrine
or living in sin,
then you don't have permission to confront him.
You need to grow up.

The Kingdom is about life
and **about building one another up,**
not tearing things and people down.

Our God is the greatest artist,
the greatest poet,
the greatest dramatist,
and the greatest director
in the universe.

When you grow in maturity,
you will start to discover that
God is very good,
very kind,
and often very funny.

But you can only discover this one way,
through this simple,
Ancient Path.

The next key is equally important:
seizing every opportunity.

The Power of Going to the Dangerous Place

Life in Babylon is awkward.

Four nice Jewish boys
are brought into the center
of the pagan wizardry
of the Babylonian court.

I don't know how they did it,
but somehow,
they remained faithful in the process.

And one day,
Nebuchadnezzar had a dream
and decided that if none of his advisors
could interpret it,
all the advisors were going to die.

Daniel
could have either seen this as a crisis
and panicked,
or an opportunity.

Once you begin to have a Kingdom perspective,
you begin to see you **always have a choice.**
You can pause,
get quiet,
and ask for God's perspective,
or you can go with your emotions,

make rash decisions,
and have drama.

And Daniel
gets quiet,
goes to the head of the guard,
and tells him
that his God
can interpret dreams.

And he does interpret the dream.
It was a crisis,
but God made it an opportunity.

I mentioned that many Christians in the arts
choose to hide out in safe places.
They go to places where the Christians are,
like Colorado Springs,
and avoid the places where the **people are,**
like London,
New York City,
Paris,
and Berlin.
And both the Christians
and the cities
suffer.

The lesson of Daniel,
and Esther for that matter,
is the power of going to the dangerous place.

Five years ago,
God called me from Boston
to London.
It has been really hard.
I still haven't sorted out housing,
and I barely make enough money to get by.
It's challenging.
It's scary.
But,
God gives me opportunities
to talk to the people who make decisions for other people.

I pray with media executives,
and get to disciple people who have an
audience in the larger art world.

It's lonely.

The Christians continually tell me it is too expensive
and that I don't have the support base to do what I do.
But God.

Every day,
I pray one simple prayer:
God,
help me see everything the enemy doesn't want me to see
and help me be in the right place at the right time.

The only way the color of the city is going to change
from the dirty gray to something better
is if the Kingdom invades.
It is all about worship
and it is all about relationship.
And you can't have relationships unless
you go where the people are.

Daniel and his companions
went the opposite of conventional wisdom.
They didn't run off to a Christian enclave somewhere.
They stayed in the court.
They didn't try to escape or fight.
It was hard,
and they had to learn all about
pagan religion,
divination,
court intrigue,
and the inside of the Babylonian world.
They learned their lessons well,
and when the moment of opportunity
arose,
Daniel could seize it.

We forget
that if they had not paid the price,

they would not have had the opportunity to
interpret the dream.
**You can only be in the right place
at the right time
if you go.**

When I was a boy,
we sang a song at school.

> *Wherever He leads I'll go,*
> *Wherever He leads I'll go,*
> *I will follow my Christ who loves me so;*
> *Wherever He leads I'll go.*

I sang it,
and I meant it.

I mentioned earlier that
the son of one of my team members was shot in Boston.
It wasn't long after the Boston bombing.
It was a hard season.
Stuff like this happens
when you go where the action is.

I called a ministry colleague for support
and he said,

"Man, you need to move down south where it's easy,
you will never build a ministry up there."

I eventually parted ways with that person.
Heidi Baker once remarked
that she wasn't building a ministry,
she was building the Kingdom;
it was God's business to build the ministry.

It is God's business to build you up.
We are back to the difference between
the Kingdom and Babylon.

When you know who you are, usually,
you know what you are supposed to do.
And if you know what you are supposed to do,

God will show you where to go.
It's back to identity.
Everything is from the inside out.

**When you know who you are,
you can walk toward the danger
and not hide from it.**

The favor Daniel received
elevated him to the head of the empire.
It was too much for him to do on his own,
and he was smart.
He asked that his friends
Shadrach,
Meshach and Abednego
be delegated to the outlying territories.
Daniel knew
that although it was dangerous
and full of intrigue,
he needed to be in the center.
He stayed at court.

Meanwhile,
his comrades discovered another very important lesson.

You cannot do it alone.

Four Men in a Furnace

When you go to the dangerous place,
you discover
that pagans act like pagans.
I learned a long time ago
not to be shocked by my friends
who were into weird religions,
wacky politics,
and kinky sex.

These folks are not believers,
and I can't expect them to act
like good evangelicals from
Wheaton.

No,
in the arts,
you are going to find a lot of things.
You are going to meet people who
not only do weird things,
but think the weird things are normal,
and they want you to do them too.

A few years ago,
God told me to start wearing a
clerical collar.
It was really hard at first,
and there are days I don't want to put it on.
And it really gets the Christians uptight.

But,
when I am walking down Brick Lane in London,
or around Southbank,
or in the pub,
people come up to me
and ask me questions.

"Why do you wear that thing?" they ask.
"Jesus told me to," I reply.
"Wow, Jesus TALKS to you!?"

                                        And that, my friends,
                            is how you become salt and light.

Even so,
life among the unbelievers
is very tricky,
and sometimes you have to be very careful.

Daniel's companions
were asked to bow down to a golden image,
and if they didn't,
Nebuchadnezzar was going to throw them into a burning, fiery furnace.

There is a war between Babylon and the Kingdom.
And these tests we keep seeing in Daniel
are all the result of palace intrigue.
If you go into the dangerous place
again and again,
**God will give you favor,
because you have a source of creativity
and inspiration
that is endless.**
The others around you do not.
And so,
their only option is to take you out.

And so,
Daniel's friends
refuse to bow down to the idol.
And they face the consequences.

Their strength
in that moment
came from the fact **they were not alone.**
And this is one of the big keys
for artists and creative people.

Let's face it:
you and I
tend to be solitary,
and somewhat competitive,
people.

As I mentioned before,
artists are like cats.
Cats do not run in herds.

And so I had to find a way to help these
fiercely independent people
come together.

The smallest unit in the British Army
is the **fire team.**

Often, this is a pair of soldiers
who go into a dangerous place
to perform a specific mission.

Jesus told us
that if two or more are gathered in his name,
he is there with them.[78]
And so,
I began running something we called
"Fire Teams."
**You only need one other person
to form a group.**

And the group is very simple.

You meet with someone else,
and you begin with a simple exercise called the Examen:
Since we met last time,
what has been your cause of consolation?

In other words,
what are you grateful for?

And then we ask another question:
"What is the source of your desolation?"
In other words,
what has caused you pain or distress?

And we might stop and pray about this.
It is a way to warm up the conversation,
but it also serves a purpose and has substance.
I hate shallow group activities, don't you?

Then we take out the Bible and read the day's Gospel lesson.
Yes,
there is that Gospel lesson again.
It is central.
**Jesus is the King of the Kingdom,
and every warrior artisan
has to be in tune to the Voice of the King.**

We do a simple exercise called "Lectio Divina."
**We read the text three times, slowly,
out loud,
and listen.**

The first time you listen for the detail that appeals to your head.
What thought did the passage evoke?
What detail stood out to you?

The second time,
we listen for what Jesus is saying to our hearts.
Is there something in there that is touching you
emotionally?
Is there something that gives you that warmth of the Holy Spirit?
Is there comfort,
or is there conviction?

And then we listen for our hands.
What is God telling us to do?

It is very simple.

**Then we sit together in silence for ten to twenty minutes,
and share what we sense the Lord saying.**
We are listening to God for each other.

And finally,
we pray for one another and go our own way.

And out of it,
I have seen my own life change
and the lives of others change.
One person said that this simple model
has taught them more about discipleship
than any other thing.

It works.
And most importantly,
it works for artists and creative people.

At the end of this book,
I will leave the outline of our Fire Team model
so you can try it out.
Daniel's friends
went into the fire.
And the guards and the emperor
looked in
and they saw
a fourth man in the fire.

You know,
the text doesn't say
Shadrach,
Meshach,
and Abednego
saw the fourth man.

**Even so,
when they stuck together,
just like Jesus promised,
he was with them.**

When you go with others,
you are greater than the sum of the parts.

**And you can do more with others
than you could ever have done alone.**

The next most important key
to succeeding in Babylon
is the daily rhythm.

Three Times a Day

Throughout the book of Daniel,
Daniel experiences a series of tests
that arose from the jealousy
of the others in the court.

This is part of a political game.
Everyone wants to get the guy at the top.
And it is also
the fact that Daniel walks with God
and that relationship
is the source of his
wisdom,
giftedness,
and favor.

You become like the one with whom you spend your time.

And someone in the court
made the connection
that Daniel
got down on his knees
three times a day
and turned his face toward Jerusalem.
**His daily rhythm
formed him
and strengthened him.**

In 1993,
I had my first exposure to
the Abbey of Gethsemani
in Trappist, Kentucky.
In those days,
I had a lot of romantic ideas
about being a monk.
And it did not take long
for me to figure out
that the cloistered life
was not for me.

I liked to talk.

Even so,
the attraction to the rhythm
of the monastic life remained.

I spent the early part of my
Christian life
in charismatic
and Pentecostal churches.
Although the
vitality and real power of God
was in that world,
there was also a lot of instability,
emotionalism,
and drama
as well.

In search of balance,
I eventually drifted into the
charismatic renewal in the
Protestant Episcopal church.
I was given a prayer book,
and I began to pray morning
and evening prayer.

Thirty years ago,
I began to use the ordered,
appointed
scripture readings,

and I began to get soaked in the Bible
several times a day.
It was this daily practice,
mostly centered in the daily offices,
**that provided the skeleton for my
spiritual life.**

One interesting thing
about being a highly creative person:
**if you are forced to invent your spiritual life
all the time,
it saps your creativity.**
I found that my prayer life
became pretty boring
when I drifted away from the
prayer book,
usually because of pressure
from my classmates and friends.

The rhythm that the prayer book provided
transformed my Christian experience
from a blob of experiences
and emotions
to a being with
a skeleton
and muscles.
I began to rise up,
walk,
and move forward.

**That forward movement
has been going on
for thirty years.**
And it works.
Of course,
I'm not a monk
and neither are you.
No matter how hard I tried,
or how guilty I felt,
there were parts of the monastic rhythm I never could embrace.

When you are a musician,
actor,
performer,
or arts professional,
you usually have evening commitments.

I've never been able to say Evening Prayer
no matter how hard I tried.

Early in the morning works,
and now is my most creative time of the day.
A brief pause for about 15 minutes
in the middle of the day happens
because we now have a prayer meeting,
but before that, I might stop for five.
And prayer before bed happens about
seventy-five percent of the time.

I'm a real person
living a real life.

The issue is not performance;
the issue is rhythm
and being shaped by the Bible
and the ongoing story that we tell
through the seasons of the year.

In the trade,
we call this
spiritual formation.
And when you get shaped this way,
it comes out in every area of your life.
You have a balance
and a steadiness just like Daniel displays
throughout his life.

This is not about performing a ritual for God.
Someone asked me about this once.
I told them I don't say my prayers for God,
I say them for me.

The goal is that my life would become a constant
commentary on my prayer book.
Do these words
really shape and change me?
Do they help me hear God
in an organic way
all the time?

Do they keep me connected to all that has gone before,
all God promises will be,
and who I am now?

We are back to worship,
and Identity
and direction.

Your inner life determines your creative output.

And again, we are back to that
daily gospel reading.
If I am in a busy day,
I hear it early in the morning,
and I hear it during a small group meeting,
and I hear it from one of the folks who touch
base with me throughout the week.

This is **how**
you get the long obedience in the same direction.

When I was a student,
we were told that John Wesley prayed
four hours a day.
They were evangelicals
so they left out the important detail:
John Wesley was a priest,
and he said
the daily offices
every day,
and that alone was about three hours.

We are given examples but no way to get there.

I had the great honor as a youth
to know a man who traveled with Smith Wigglesworth.
And he told me the things you don't find in books.
He arose at five every morning,
opened his Bible,
prayed,
and took communion.
As a discipline,
he never went more than twenty minutes without
reading the Bible and praying.
This is how he learned to have faith.

Learning a rhythm
is how I got here.
I learned to pray the Psalms from a book
(and with the internet).
My daily prayer rhythm
is where my walk of faith comes from,
where the miracles have their root,
where the Friday emails come from,
all the books,
teaching,
podcasts,
and workshops.

And this rhythm is a discipline,
but it is not a drudgery,
and it is not hard.
It's very simple,
and it works.

At the end of the book
I have included a basic skeleton,
and resources
so you can start on this journey.

Developing a daily rhythm
is one of the most creative things
you can do.

These are the tools you need to become an
elite warrior artisan
fighting within Babylon.

Remember,
Babylon is your enemy.
Babylon is not safe.
Babylon is not home.
And most importantly,
Babylon
is
doomed.

Babylon is Doomed

One of the most influential films of all time
is Fritz Lang's *Metropolis*.

Like a lot of film nerds,
I watched badly cut copies of it
on fuzzy VHS tapes in the 1980s and '90s.
I will never forget
seeing the full restoration
with the original orchestral score,
and for the first time,
understanding that the story was Biblical.

You have probably seen the sequence
when the mad doctor Rotwang
creates a robot woman in his laboratory.

In the restoration,
the famous transformation scene
of the robot woman
is clearly a satanic ritual,
and the woman that was created
was the great whore, Babylon.

This book began
with a road in the wilderness.
And then we saw an apocalyptic battle
between global powers
and the army of artisans.

Then we turned to the ultimate
warrior artisan,
David.
He brought about a worship revolution,
and received a promise of a throne.
And finally,
we have learned from Daniel
how he managed a cataclysmic shift
within enemy territory.

Eventually,
all empires
experience the same end.

The end of the story of Daniel's life
comes
when, as an old man,
he is summoned to read the
proverbial writing on the wall.
And the writing says,
you have been measured
and you have been found wanting,
and your empire is coming to an end.
And all the condemnations of Babylon,
the once-great city,
have now come to pass.

Today, Babylon is a barren plot of earth
in the middle of Iraq.

Throughout scripture,
Babylon came to represent
not just the empire that destroyed the temple,
but also the system of this world.
Babylon is the commander
of the four horns in Zechariah.
It is the same enemy
and the same source of power.
The army of the four horns is a demonic army
spreading lies to make you discouraged,
afraid,
and unable to lift your head.

Babylon is not home.
Babylon is not safe.
And Babylon is a system.

The book of Revelation
personifies Babylon as a woman.
She is a whore who the
political,
economic,
and cultural leaders of the earth
gladly copulate with
in order to benefit from her power.
She feeds on the blood of the martyrs,
and she rides on the back of the beast.

In the old Book of Common Prayer,
we prayed,
"from the world, the flesh and the devil,
good Lord, deliver us."

Babylon is the world.
She is far more dangerous than the devil.
She is bloodthirsty,
and wherever the earth mother is worshiped,
there is a thirst for human blood.
Whether it be child sacrifice or abortion.

> Then a mighty angel picked up a boulder the size of a huge
> millstone. He threw it into the ocean and shouted,
> "Just like this, the great city Babylon
>   will be thrown down with violence
>   and will never be found again.
> The sound of harps, singers, flutes, and trumpets
>   will never be heard in you again.
> No craftsmen and no trades
>   will ever be found in you again.
> The sound of the mill
>   will never be heard in you again.
> The light of a lamp
>   will never shine in you again.
> The happy voices of brides and grooms
>   will never be heard in you again.

> For your merchants were the greatest in the world,
>> and you deceived the nations with your sorceries.
> In your streets flowed the blood of the prophets and of God's holy people
>> and the blood of people slaughtered all over the world."[79]

Revelation 18 tells us that Babylon
is a political system
and a commercial system
and a **cultural artistic system.**

It is the system of the global power of the four horns.
And there is only one way to overcome this
power.

Come out of her.

We live in an illusion
that there are "fifty shades of grey"
between good and evil.
No.
There is only good and evil.
There is only one Kingdom of God,
and one Babylon.
There is no middle country
where you can live in both.
We who live in the realm of creators
know that we have access
to more than one source of inspiration.
We can draw from the well of life
or the cistern of satan.
It really is that simple.

We are living in one of the most tumultuous times
in recorded history.
The technological change
is happening so fast
that even those who understand it
cannot keep up.
And like the description of Babylon
in Revelation,
the system of this world

seems to be increasingly demonic
and consumed with trafficking in human souls.
The masks are off.

But,
this dangerous time,
as we have learned,
is also a time of opportunity.

We are
really in a war.

War is hell.
People's lives are lost,
and people die.
Sometimes,
like the American Civil War,
we are pitted
brother against brother.
Jesus said he came not to bring peace on the earth,
but rather,
to make enemies of your own household.[80]

It's great to have a successful art career.
Some of you reading this
are content
to sell cards or your prints,
go to art fairs,
or market a painting here and there.

I am not faulting that.
Those endeavors are fine in a time of peace.
This is not a time of peace.

In a time of war,
you have to think strategically.
You have to be wise as a serpent,
and harmless as a dove.[81]
Some of you reading this
have settled far below your calling.
Others of you
have bought into a system

that is ultimately
the enemy of the Kingdom.

In 1999, a colleague said that
the day was coming when listening to God,
and knowing when to turn right
or turn left
would be the difference between
living and dying.

This is the day of which he spoke.

Many of you have spent time at conferences,
and many of you have consumed a lot of prophetic
stuff on the internet.
In parts of the world,
religious entertainment is acceptable.
Sadly,
a lot of it
flows from Babylon.

If you have made it this far,
you know that you are called
to the company of warrior artists.

In the book of Revelation,
Babylon is destroyed
before
Jesus returns.

What does this mean to us?
It means
that we who are called to live
in a time of change,
transition,
and trials,
are fighting a winning battle.

We are going to win.
We are going to succeed.
We are going to overcome.

And how do we do this?
Learn to recognize the voice of God.
Listen to the Lord and do what he tells you.
Grow in maturity within a company of others.
Build a solid rhythm that keeps you
in conscious contact with God every day.
This is how you develop focus
and this is how you become a warrior artisan.

The rest,
like your skill development,
career choices,
and work ethic
are just details.
I trust God
and trust you
to make the right choices.

When you do this,
then you can join the victory song:

> After this I heard
> what seemed to be
> the mighty voice
> of a great multitude in heaven, crying,
> "Hallelujah!
> Salvation and glory and power belong to our God,
> for his judgments are true and just;
> he has judged the great harlot
> who corrupted the earth with her fornication,
> and he has avenged on her the blood of his servants."
>
> Once more they cried,
> "Hallelujah!
> The smoke from her goes up for ever and ever."
> And the twenty-four elders
> and the four living creatures fell down
> and worshiped God who is seated on the throne,
> saying,
> "Amen. Hallelujah!"

And from the throne came a voice crying,
"Praise our God, all you his servants,
you who fear him, small and great."

Then I heard
what seemed to be the voice of a great multitude,
like the sound of many waters
and like the sound of mighty thunder peals,
crying,
"Hallelujah!
For the Lord our God the Almighty reigns.
Let us rejoice and exult and give him the glory,
for the marriage of the Lamb has come,
and his Bride has made herself ready."[82]

A Throne in the Earth

The end of Daniel
is concerned with a series of apocalyptic visions.
In the seventh chapter,
we see horns again,
and one of them is making a lot of noise.

> And in the midst of this,
> thrones are brought in
> and the Ancient of Days
> takes his seat.
>
> and behold, with the clouds of heaven
>   there came one like a son of man,
> and he came to the Ancient of Days
>   and was presented before him.
>
> And to him was given dominion
>   and glory and kingdom,
> that all peoples, nations, and languages
>   should serve him;
> his dominion is an everlasting dominion,
>   which shall not pass away,
> and his kingdom one
>   that shall not be destroyed.[83]

Jesus only referred to himself
as the Son of Man,
and there is an interesting parallel

to this vision
and the beginning of the book of Acts.

> So when they had come together, they asked him, "Lord, will you at this time restore the kingdom to Israel?" He said to them, "It is not for you to know times or seasons which the Father has fixed by his own authority. But you shall receive power when the Holy Spirit has come upon you; and you shall be my witnesses in Jerusalem and in all Judea and Samaria and to the end of the earth." And when he had said this, as they were looking on, he was lifted up, and a cloud took him out of their sight. And while they were gazing into heaven as he went, behold, two men stood by them in white robes, and said, "Men of Galilee, why do you stand looking into heaven? This Jesus, who was taken up from you into heaven, will come in the same way as you saw him go into heaven."[84]

The Apostles
were certain by this point
that Jesus was the **heir of David**
and that his Kingdom
and all the promises to David
would be fulfilled.

And Jesus
instead
tells them to wait
and be filled with the Holy Spirit,
and the promise is given
that the Son of Man
is going to return in the cloud,
just as he left.

In 2006, God called me to
"Raise up an army of artists
who will build Jesus a throne
in the earth."

That's pretty cryptic.

We all know that these are unusual times.
I can say this for certain:

Jesus is coming back sooner than any of us may realize.
This shift in history
might be the last one.
Regardless,
we are called to be like the ten wise virgins
who had oil in their lamps.
We are to be filled with the Holy Spirit,
and be bright and lit up
for the King when he comes.
The King is coming.

**And this King is going to sit
on the throne promised to David.**

If you are a believer in Jesus the Messiah,
you have been brought
not only into the family of God,
but the family of David.

We are his throne.

The book of Zechariah ends with this promise:

> On that day the Lord will put a shield about the inhabitants of Jerusalem so that the feeblest among them on that day shall be like David, and the house of David shall be like God, like the angel of the Lord, at their head.[85]

Every warrior
artist for the Kingdom
is called to be like the mighty men of David
who did exploits.
Some of you are called to step out in faith and see
God meet and provide for you in ways that exceed expectations.
Some of you are called to have big platforms
and footprints
that will give you a voice to those who would otherwise
never hear the gospel.
Some of you are called to raise up the fallen and brokenhearted.
Some of you are called to discover new solutions
for the myriad of problems that plague cities and nations.
Some of you are simply called to do something beautiful for God.

And all of us,
literally
or symbolically,
are being summoned to the mountain of the Lord.
And out of that multitude,
we will be chosen
as Levites and priests,
to bring about a worship revolution.
A new sound
and the release of the light and color of heaven.

In the 1980s,
Don Moen wrote a song
that has become sort of the anthem of our community.

> *Jesus,*
> *we enthrone you.*
> *We proclaim you are King.*
> *Standing here*
> *in the midst of us,*
> *we raise you up with our praise.*
> *And as we worship, build a throne,*
> *and as we worship, build a throne,*
> *and as we worship, build a throne,*
> *Come Lord Jesus,*
> *and take your place.*[86]

There is only one King of the Kingdom.

Our job
is to build a place for him
in our lives,
in the cultures of this world,
and to bring about a cultural
and an arts revolution
so that the Kingdoms of this world
can become
the Kingdoms of our Lord and of his Christ.

Part IV

A WAY FORWARD

The End of the Pilgrimage

This book
began in the woods,
remember?

There was a road in the wilderness.
Some on the road understood the times they lived in,
but most did not.
And some
lagged behind.

This wilderness is just that.
I didn't mention that there were trails that led
off into different directions.
Some of them were wide and pleasant,
but they led to dens of bandits,
and other pleasant-looking paths
led you over dangerous cliffs
and to a nasty demise.

I didn't mention
that there were tricksters
and snake oil salesmen along the way.
And I didn't mention
the hookers,
the pushers,
and the sideshow carnivals
that somehow
"set up shop" along the road.

No one knows how they got there.

And way up front,
there are still the tenacious few
blazing a trail
way ahead of the crowd.

They know something
that the pack who lags
behind the times
really never understood.

The crowd thinks this is a journey.
The odd thing about journeys
is they often have no point
and have no goal.
A lot of journeys are just that,
a season of travel with no clear destination.
There is no urgency,
and often,
a journey gets misdirected
by the mundane events of life.

Those
brave,
adventurous,
creative,
and artistic
souls ahead—
those prophets—
know
that this is not a journey.

This is a pilgrimage.

The road that we are building through the wilderness
is the pilgrim pathway to a
city,
and that city is on a mountain.

We are going somewhere.
This isn't just a cycle;

there is a destination.
And there is a price that must be paid
to get there.
This pilgrimage is costly.

This city is made by the Author of Beauty,
the Divine Designer,
the Creative Source of the Universe.
And this city
is the place
where all the kings of the earth,
and all the cultures of the earth,
bring their best.

The best food,
the best clothes,
the best songs,
the best plays,
the finest music,
the most glorious art,
and the most refined
and elegant of manners.

They are cutting a path in the wilderness
to get home.

And when they get there,
there will be no night,
no temple,
no intermediary.
Because they know
they are the temple.
And they will talk with God
face to face,
as with a friend.

Stay focused.
Keep going.
Don't give up.

This
war
is
worth
winning.

The last few chapters of this book
are the practical things you can do.
These are the things I have used for thirty years,
and the things I have shared with our community.
It is the map
that I use
to stay on the Ancient Pathway.

Develop a rhythm.
Do good work.
Run toward the danger.
And listen to the Lord and do what he tells you.

The Ancient Pathways:
A Prayer Rhythm for Artists

A few years ago,
I was attending a conference where they sang
the verse from a long forgotten gospel song:

> *Oh, for the floods on the thirsty land!*
> *Oh, for a mighty revival!*
> *Oh, for a sanctified, fearless band,*
> *Ready to hail its arrival!*

The idea of raising up an army of artists
can become abstract
and vague.
From experience,
people project onto our community
their preconceived notions
of what artists,
arts,
and community should look like.

If I get told God wants me to form a hippy commune
one more time,
I will gag.

After I heard that little song,
our community began to pray a more specific prayer:
"God, send us a million
sanctified
and fearless artists."

At the end of this book,
I want to leave you with some practices you can put in place
that will help you become those two things:

holy
and focused.

Many of us have been taught
that in order to become holy,
we need to embrace morality,
and try hard to maintain it.
And then God will make you be holy.

Some of us have been taught that if we have an encounter
with the Holy Spirit,
we will receive an impartation of holiness.
And then we have to maintain it ourselves
in our own strength.

In other words,
holiness is something we need to try to achieve
and then God will help us.

And of course,
this is impossible.

Most of you know this approach
is like holding sand in your fist.
Eventually, it all runs out
and you are left right where you started.

And so, when someone finds out that you failed,
the church turns on you.
The cancer of imperfection must be removed.
This is the heart of religion:
"I must do something to get something from God."
As much as these folks preach grace,
in practice,
there is very little.
Paul admonishes us
in Romans 12:1-2:

> I appeal to you therefore, brethren, by the mercies of God, to present your bodies as a living sacrifice, holy and acceptable to God, which is your spiritual worship. Do not be conformed to this world but be transformed by the renewal of your mind,

>   that you may prove what is the will of God, what is good and
>   acceptable and perfect.

Paul is telling us that in the New Covenant,
true worship is presenting our bodies
as living sacrifices to God.

In Leviticus,
we are told that the process of bringing
an animal to the Lord as an offering
makes the animal holy.
The animal did nothing to make itself holy.
As a sacrifice,
it **became** holy.[87]

At the beginning of this book,
I quoted Jesus,
who calls all of us
to take up our cross and to follow him,
and to die daily.
Like Paul,
Jesus is asking us
to join our offering with his,
and to embrace the cross—
death to our own way—
in exchange for his.
And in doing this,
a transformation will begin to occur.
We will be made holy.
When we present our bodies as living sacrifices,
our bodies become Temples of the Holy Spirit.
This is not a one time event.
And this is why so many of us fail
in the area of holiness.

Holiness is like the manna
that fell upon Israel in the desert.
It was only good for a day.
You cannot live on yesterday's manna.
You cannot count on yesterday's holiness for today.
As an artist, I was taught that
you are only as good as your last audition,

your last performance,
your last painting.
This is why you need to always grow and learn.
You cannot achieve holiness through your own effort.
All you can do is this:

> **Father,**
> **I offer you my body today**
> **as a living sacrifice.**
> **This is my spiritual worship.**
> **I ask you to send your fire to consume the offering,**
> **make me holy,**
> **and help me embrace your perfect will.**

And that prayer is good.
But it is only good for today.
Tomorrow, you will have to pray it again.
Just like in Alcoholics Anonymous,
you only have
one
day
at a
time.

That is why both Paul and Jesus say
to take up your cross daily.
And in doing this,
you stop being religious
and begin being holy.
This is how you begin to be a new creation.
The old is gone,
and the new has come.

Holiness is only half the equation.
In order to be a warrior artist,
you also have to be fearless and focused.
And this is where I see people lose steam and momentum.

Sometime in the last few centuries,
religion—and Christianity in particular—
went from being the bedrock on which you build your life
to an activity you pursue in your leisure time.

And in the United States,
that leisurely pursuit of religion
has evolved into something called
"Consumer Christianity."
In other words,
religious activity as entertainment.

And so,
new churches are built to look like theatres or concert venues.
There is big money in entertainment,
and bigger money in religion.
You combine those two things
and you have a **deadly, addictive substance.**
It looks like a God thing,
but it's not.
And so people
think that the feelings you get from being at a big event
designed to manipulate your emotions
are the Holy Spirit.
And when the feelings stop,
so does the devotion.

In golf,
there is an important concept
called **"follow through."**
When you swing to hit the ball,
you don't abruptly stop after you hit the ball.
No,
you keep swinging until the arc of the swing is finished.
The follow through is actually the most important part,
because the goal of the swing is to hit the ball the furthest,
and the best way to do that is to create a powerful arc.

Many Christians are terrible at follow through.
If you want to make a difference,
succeed in Babylon,
and bring about a mighty Christian revolution,
you need to stay focused
after you "hit the ball."
You have to continue
every day
to become excellent.

**Developing a rhythm of prayer
is how you develop a powerful arc
of holiness and focus in your life.**

You can't become holy by doing things,
but the things you do will make you holy.

This is why Paul said
that you offer your body,
and then you renew your mind.
The renewing of your mind
will work outwardly,
what God does inwardly.
**You become a sacrament:
an outward sign of an inward grace.**
Your work becomes a sacrament.
Your life is an expression.
When you commit to this way of life,
you suddenly find yourself at odds
with the majority of Christians around you.
So much of what is taught is a commitment to mediocrity.
People are rewarded for saying "it's all good,"
when most of it is below the standard.

If you have made it this far,
you have begun to discover that we really are in a war.
We need artists and creative people
 who will not bow to the mediocrity of our age.

You will never win a war
if you think that the things that put us in this mess
are good.
God is looking for those who will worship him
in spirit and in truth.
It is all about worship.
And worship
is first surrendering to God every day.
It is second
getting into the Bible and developing a rhythm of prayer
that overrides the programming
from the world,
the flesh, and the devil.

And third,
it requires you to find other
focused,
tenacious
warriors,
who are also called to bring the Kingdom of God
from heaven to earth.

This last section is how.
How do I get there?

You need a road map,
and you need to learn a life of prayer,
and how to listen to God.

The last section of this book
contains the things I really use.
They are adapted from the monastic prayer model
I learned from monks
thirty years ago.
Their example of
silence,
solitude,
and discipline
inspired me
and determined the direction of my life.

And this model
works
when you are living a creative life
and working a real job.

Members of our Belonging House fellowship
use these prayers,
and the ones who take it seriously
see transformation in their lives.

Theory is useless in a war.
These are weapons you can use.

I lead an ecumenical community,
and my own tradition is one that honors Mary.
If references to Mary and the saints are not your tradition,
feel free to overlook them.

Love one another.

Prayer in the Morning

Some guidance on the marks throughout this portion of the book. Things marked with (+) indicate where you may make the sign of the cross. Bold print indicates group responses when you are praying in a group.

O Lord, open our lips;
And our mouth shall proclaim your praise.
Glory be to the Father, and to the Son, and to the Holy Spirit,
as it was in the beginning, is now and ever shall be, world without end. Amen.

Alleluia! (omitted in Lent)

Come let us sing to the Lord;
   let us shout for joy to the Rock of our salvation.
Let us come before his presence with thanksgiving
   and raise a loud shout to him with psalms.
For the Lord is a great God,
   and a great King above all gods.
In his hand are the caverns of the earth,
   and the heights of the hills are his also.
The sea is his, for he made it,
   and his hands have molded the dry land.
Come, let us bow down, and bend the knee,
   and kneel before the Lord our Maker.
For he is our God,
   and we are the people of his pasture and the sheep of his hand.
Oh, that today you would hearken to his voice!

Or:
Christ our Passover has been sacrificed for us,
   so let us celebrate the feast,
Not with the old leaven of corruption and wickedness
   but with the unleavened bread of sincerity and truth.
Christ once raised from the dead dies no more;
   death has no more dominion over him.
In dying, he died to sin once for all;
   in living, he lives to God.
See yourselves, therefore, as dead to sin

   and alive to God in Jesus Christ our Lord.
Christ has been raised from the dead;
   the first fruits of those who sleep.
For since by one man came death,
   by another has come also the resurrection of the dead,
For as in Adam all die,
   even so in Christ shall all be made alive.

A HYMN may be sung.

Lord God, almighty and everlasting Father,
you have brought us in safety to this new day:
Set our hearts on fire with the glory of your Holy Spirit.
Open our ears to hear your word.
Strengthen our souls to do your will.
Empower us to overcome in every circumstance,
and in all we do, help us to fulfill your purpose,
through Jesus Christ our Lord. Amen.

The Daily Readings

A lesson from the Old Testament or the Epistles.
The Psalm for the Day.
The daily Gospel.

Take a few moments to read the gospel.
Then return to it.

What is Jesus saying to you that stands out?
Pause.

Read it again.
What is the Lord saying to your heart?
Pause again.

What is the Lord asking you to do?
Take a few minutes to sit with the Lord.
Lord, what is on your agenda today?
Lord, who do you want to be for me today?
Lord, how are you praying for me today?

O Holy Spirit,
beloved of my soul,
I adore You.
Enlighten me, guide me, strengthen me, console me.
Tell me what I should do.
Give me your orders.
I promise to submit myself
to all that You desire of me
and accept all that You permit to happen to me.
Let me only know Your will.[88]

Take some time to write down what the Lord is saying today.

Blessed be the Lord, the God of Israel;
   he has come to his people and set them free.
He has raised up for us a mighty savior,
   born of the house of his servant David.
Through his holy prophets he promised of old,
that he would save us from our enemies,
   from the hands of all who hate us.
He promised to show mercy to our fathers
   and to remember his holy covenant.
This was the oath he swore to our father Abraham,
   to set us free from the hands of our enemies,
Free to worship him without fear,
   holy and righteous in his sight
   all the days of our life.
You, my child, shall be called the prophet of the Most High,
   for you will go before the Lord to prepare his way,
To give his people knowledge of salvation
   by the forgiveness of their sins.
In the tender compassion of our God
   the dawn from on high shall break upon us,
To shine on those who dwell in darkness and the shadow of death,
   and to guide our feet into the way of peace.
Glory to the Father, and to the Son, and to the Holy Spirit:
   as it was in the beginning, is now, and will be for ever. Amen.

The Prayers

Lord, have mercy.
Christ, have mercy.
Lord, have mercy.

Save your people, Lord, and bless your inheritance,
Govern and uphold them now and always.
Day by day, we bless you;
We praise your name for ever.
Keep us today, Lord, from all sin;
Have mercy on us, Lord, have mercy.
Lord, show us your love and mercy,
For we put our trust in you.
In you, Lord, is our hope:
Let us never hope in vain.

At this time, bring before the Lord the persons
and things that concern you,
and leave them with Him.

**Lord Jesus Christ,
you stretched out your arms of love
on the hard wood of the cross
that everyone might come within
the reach of your saving embrace:
So clothe us in your Spirit that we,
reaching forth our hands in love,
may bring those who do not know you
to the knowledge and love of you;
for the honor of your Name. Amen.**

**Father of us all
who rules and reigns within the heavens,
may your name be made holy among all nations.
Come, Kingdom of God.
Be done, will of God,
on earth as that will is unhindered in heaven.
Give us today our supersubstantial bread.
Forgive us our trespasses
as we forgive those who sin against us.
Lead us away from trials,**

and deliver us from the evil one.
For the Kingdom,
the power,
and the Glory are yours
now and forever. Amen.

On feast days, the following is added:

We praise you, O God:
We acclaim you as the Lord;
All creation worships you,
the Father everlasting.
To you all angels, all the powers of heaven:
the cherubim and seraphim sing in endless praise,
Holy, Holy, Holy, Lord! God of power and might.
Heaven and earth are full of your glory.
The glorious company of apostles praise you.
The noble fellowship of prophets praise you.
The white-robed army of martyrs praise you.
Throughout the world, the Holy Church acclaims you.
Father, of majesty unbounded;
Your true and only Son, worthy of all praise;
the Holy Spirit, Advocate and Guide.
You, Christ, are the King of Glory:
the eternal Son of the Father.
When you took our flesh to set us free,
You humbly chose the Virgin's womb.
You overcame the sting of death,
and opened the kingdom of heaven to all believers.
You are seated at God's right hand in glory;
and we believe you will come to be our judge.
Come then, Lord, and help your people,
bought with the price of your own blood,
and bring us with all your saints,
into glory everlasting. Amen.

The Blessing

Glory to God whose power, working in us, can do infinitely more than we can ask or imagine: Glory to him from generation to generation in the Church, and in Christ Jesus for ever and ever. Amen. (Ephesians 3:20,21)

I clothe myself with the Lord Jesus Christ,
and make no provision for the flesh.
I put myself within the Name of the Lord our God.
I put on the helmet of salvation and
the breastplate of righteousness.
I gird up my loins with the belt of truth.
I shod my feet with the preparedness of the Gospel of peace.
I take up the shield of faith,
and the sword of the spirit, which is the word of God.

May the Lord bless us and prosper us,
in the name of the Father, Son, and Holy Spirit. Amen.

The Following additional prayers for protection may be added:

I take authority over all witchcraft:
all hexes, spells, curses, or assignments sent against me.
I take authority over all hoodoo, voodoo, sex magick, soulish prayers,
false words of prophecy, and Christian prayers not from the Lord.
Jesus Christ became a curse for me on the cross,
so that I may enter into the blessing of Abraham,
whom God blessed in all things.
I break all curses from operating in my life no matter the source.
I bless those who curse me with the blood of Jesus.
I bless you, who curse me, with a holy fear of the Lord.
I bless you with a conviction of sin, an awareness of eternity, angelic
visitation, and an awareness of the cross of Christ.
I commend you to Almighty God
and rest in his complete
and total protection over my life,
my family, my work,
and all we undertake for his great name. Amen.

Prayer Throughout the Day

There are three methods that have been useful for our community in developing a rhythm of prayer without ceasing. These can be done in the midst of work or travel.

Prayer Walking
The practice of walking land, territory, or physical property and praying for God's intervention is as ancient as the march around the walls of Jericho.

Prayer walking involves engaging the world, interceding on behalf of your community, and meditating on scripture. My method of prayer walking has developed over time, but has proven to be effective in its simplicity.

Using rosary beads, or even your fingers, say the following, beginning with the larger bead:
Our Father . . .
On the smaller beads,
repeat one of these or other short aspirations as you walk.
Lord, let your kingdom come,
and your will be done, on earth as it is in heaven.

Let it be to me according to your Word.

With You, all things are possible.

My meat is to do the will of him who sent me.

If I be lifted up, I will draw all men to me.

Pray in the Spirit
As a community, we stop at midday
and pray together in tongues for fifteen minutes.
Throughout the day, in pauses from work,
we also stop and pray,
to focus on our Lord Jesus,
and keep the Incarnation central to our life and work.
The work of the artist is patterned after the life of Jesus,
son of Joseph the Artisan,
and Mary, who literally in her body,
made the Word flesh.

The Angelus, or another prayer, may be said during the day.

The Angelus
The Angel of the Lord declared unto Mary
And she conceived by the Holy Spirit.

Hail Mary, full of grace, the Lord is with you.
Blessèd are you among women,
and blessèd is the fruit of your womb, Jesus.
Holy Mary, Mother of God,
pray for us sinners, now, and at the hour of our death.

"Behold, the handmaid of the Lord;
Let it be to me according to your word."
Hail Mary . . .

The Word became flesh
And dwelt among us.
Hail Mary . . .

Pray for us, O holy Mother of God,
That we may be made worthy of the promises of Christ.

Let us pray.
We ask you, O Lord, to pour your grace into our hearts;
that as we have known the incarnation of your Son, Jesus Christ,
by the message of an angel,
so by his cross and passion
we may be brought to the glory of his resurrection;
through Jesus Christ our Lord. Amen.

Night Prayer

The Lord almighty grant us a peaceful night and a perfect end. Amen.

Be sober, be vigilant, for your enemy the devil prowls around like a roaring lion, seeking someone whom he may devour. Resist him, being firm in your faith. (1 Peter 5:8)

Our help is in the name of the Lord,
Who made heaven and earth.

Take a few minutes to sit silently and reflect on the past day.
What has been your source of thankfulness and your source of grief today?

Almighty God, our heavenly Father:
We have sinned against you,
through our own fault,
in our thoughts, and words, and actions,
and in what we have failed to do.
For the sake of your Son our Lord Jesus Christ,
forgive us all our offenses;
and grant that we may serve you
in newness of life,
to the glory of your Name. Amen.

or:
I confess to Almighty God,
to Blessed Mary ever Virgin,
to Blessed Michael the Archangel,
to Blessed John the Baptist,
to the holy Apostles Peter and Paul and to all the Saints,
that I have sinned exceedingly in thought, word, and deed;
through my fault, through my fault, through my own most grievous fault.
Therefore I beseech Blessed Mary ever Virgin,
Blessed Michael the Archangel,
Blessed John the Baptist,
the holy Apostles Peter and Paul and all the Saints,
to pray for me to the Lord our God. Amen.

+May Almighty God grant us forgiveness of all our sins, and the grace and comfort of the Holy Spirit. Amen.

O God, make speed to save us.
O Lord, make haste to help us.
Glory be to the Father, and to the Son, and to the Holy Spirit;
    as it was in the beginning, is now, and ever shall be, world without end. Amen.

Alleluia! (may be omitted in Lent)

Before the ending of the day,
Creator of the world, we pray
That you, with steadfast love, would keep
Your watch around us while we sleep.

From evil dreams defend our sight,
From fears and terrors of the night;
Tread under foot our deadly foe
That we no sinful thought may know.

O Father, that we ask be done
Through Jesus Christ, your only Son;
And Holy Spirit, by whose breath
Our souls are raised to life from death. Amen.
— St. Ambrose

PSALM 4
Answer me when I call, O God, defender of my cause;
    you set me free when I am hard-pressed;
have mercy on me and hear my prayer.
    "You mortals, how long will you dishonor my glory;
how long will you worship dumb idols and run after false gods?"
    Know that the Lord does wonders for the faithful;
when I call upon the Lord, he will hear me.
    Tremble, then, and do not sin;
speak to your heart in silence upon your bed.
    Offer the appointed sacrifices
and put your trust in the Lord.
    Many are saying, "O that we might see better times!"
Lift up the light of your countenance upon us, O Lord.
    You have put gladness in my heart,
more than when grain and wine and oil increase.
    I lie down in peace; at once I fall asleep;
for only you, Lord, make me dwell in safety.

Glory be to the Father, and to the Son, and to the Holy Spirit;
   as it was in the beginning, is now, and ever shall be, world without end. Amen.

PSALM 91
He who dwells in the shelter of the Most High,
   abides under the shadow of the Almighty.
He shall say to the Lord, "You are my refuge and my stronghold,
   my God in whom I put my trust."
He shall deliver you from the snare of the hunter
   and from the deadly pestilence.
He shall cover you with his pinions,
and you shall find refuge under his wings;
   his faithfulness shall be a shield and buckler.
You shall not be afraid of any terror by night,
   nor of the arrow that flies by day;
Of the plague that stalks in the darkness,
   nor of the sickness that lays waste at midday.
A thousand shall fall at your side and ten thousand at your right hand,
   but it shall not come near you.
Your eyes have only to behold
   to see the reward of the wicked.
Because you have made the Lord your refuge,
   and the Most High your habitation.
There shall no evil happen to you,
   neither shall any plague come near your dwelling.
For he shall give his angels charge over you,
   to keep you in all your ways.
They shall bear you in their hands,
   lest you dash your foot against a stone.
You shall tread upon the lion and adder;
   you shall trample the young lion and the serpent under your feet.
Because he is bound to me in love, therefore will I deliver him;
   I will protect him, because he knows my name.
He shall call upon me and I will answer him;
   I am with him in trouble, will rescue him and bring him to honor.
With long life will I satisfy him,
   and show him my salvation
Glory be to the Father, and to the Son, and to the Holy Spirit;
   as it was in the beginning, is now, and ever shall be, world without end. Amen.

PSALM 134
Behold now, bless the Lord, all you servants of the Lord,
  you that stand by night in the house of the Lord.
Lift up your hands in the holy place and bless the Lord;
  the Lord who made heaven and earth bless you out of Zion.
Glory be to the Father, and to the Son, and to the Holy Spirit;
  as it was in the beginning, is now, and ever shall be, world without end. Amen.

A READING (one of the following or some other)

O Lord, You are in the midst of us, and we are called by your name. Leave us not O Lord, Our God. (Jeremiah 14:9)

Come to me, all who labor and are heavy laden, and I will give you rest. Take my yoke upon you and learn from me; for I am gentle and lowly in heart and you will find rest for your souls. For my yoke is easy and my burden is light. (Matthew 11:28-30)

There remains a sabbath rest for the people of God; for those who enter God's rest also cease from their labors, as God did. Let us, therefore, strive to enter that rest. (Hebrews 4:9-11a)

Finally, beloved, whatever is true, whatever is honorable, whatever is just, whatever is pure, whatever is lovely, whatever is gracious, if there is any excellence and if there is anything worthy of praise, think about these things. What you have learned and received and heard and seen in me, do, and the God of peace will be with you. (Philippians 4:8-9)

God has not destined us to the terrors of judgment but to the full attainment of salvation through our Lord Jesus Christ, who died for us, so that whether we wake or sleep, we might live with him. (1 Thessalonians 5:9-10)

Into your hands, O Lord,
I commend my spirit. (Alleluia! Alleluia!)
For you have redeemed me, Lord God of truth.
Glory to the Father, and to the Son, and to the Holy Spirit:
Keep me as the apple of your eye.
Hide me under the shadow of your wings.

Save us, O Lord, while waking,
and guard us while sleeping,
that awake we may watch with Christ,
and asleep may rest in peace.

Now, Lord, you let your servant go in peace:
your word has been fulfilled.
My own eyes have seen the salvation
which you have prepared in the sight of every people;
A light to reveal you to the nations
and the glory of your people Israel.
Glory be to the Father, and to the Son, and to the Holy Spirit;
  as it was in the beginning, is now, and ever shall be, world without
  end. Amen.

Save us, O Lord, while waking,
and guard us while sleeping,
that awake we may watch with Christ,
and asleep may rest in peace.

The Prayers

Lord have mercy,
Christ have mercy,
Lord have mercy.

Let us pray,

Lighten our darkness,
Lord, we pray;
and in your great mercy defend us
from all perils and dangers of this night;
for the love of your only Son,
our Savior Jesus Christ. Amen.

Be present, O merciful God,
and protect us through the hours of this night,
so that we who are wearied
by the changes and chances of this life
may rest in your eternal changelessness;
through Jesus Christ our Lord. Amen.

Visit this house, O Lord, we pray,
drive far from it all the snares of the enemy;
may your holy angels dwell with us
and guard us in peace
and may your blessing be always upon us;
through Jesus Christ our Lord. Amen.

Keep watch, dear Lord,
with those who work, or watch, or weep this night,
and give your angels charge over those who sleep.
Tend the sick, Lord Christ;
give rest to the weary,
bless the dying, soothe suffering, pity the afflicted,
and all for your love's sake. Amen.

Father of us all,
who rules and reigns within the heavens,
may your name be made holy among all nations.
Come, Kingdom of God.
Be done, will of God,
on earth as that will is unhindered in heaven.
Give us today our supersubstantial bread.
Forgive us our trespasses
as we forgive those who sin against us.
Lead us away from trials,
and deliver us from the evil one.
For the Kingdom, the power, and the Glory are yours
now and forever. Amen.

In peace, we will lie down and sleep;
For you alone, Lord, make us dwell in safety.
Abide with us, Lord Jesus,
For the night is at hand and the day is now past.
As the night-watch looks for the morning,
So do we look for you, O Christ.
Come with the dawning of the day
And make yourself known in the breaking of the bread.

May the +Name of Jesus the Son of God,
which is mightier than all the hosts of Satan
and more glorious than all the hosts of heaven,
abide with you in your going out and your coming in.
By day and night, at morning and at evening,
at all times and in all places may it protect and defend you.
From the wrath of evildoers,
from the assaults of evil spirits,
from foes visible and invisible,
from the snares of the devil,
from all passions that beguile the soul and body:
may it guard, protect and deliver you. Amen.[89]

And May Almighty God, +Father, Son, and Holy Spirit,
bless and watch over us, now and forever. Amen.

Traditionally we honor Mary after the blessing.

Into his joy, the Lord has received you,
Virgin God-bearer, Mother of Christ.

You have beheld the King in his beauty,
Mary, daughter of Israel.

You have made answer for the creation
To the redeeming will of God.

Light, fire and life, divine and immortal,
Joined to our nature you have brought forth,

That to the glory of God the Father,
Heaven and earth might be restored.[90]

The Fire Team

Engaging Each Other

Since our last meeting,
What is the thing that gave you consolation?
What is the thing that brought you desolation?

Engaging the Imagination

Lectio Divina
Before the meeting, each member of the group should read and reflect on the week's gospel lesson.

Read the passage three times slowly together.
What do you hear God speaking to your head?
What do you hear God saying to your heart?
What do you think God is asking you to do in response?

During the group meeting, read the passage, and ask these questions again.

Engaging the Holy Spirit

Spend 7-10 minutes in silence.
Share what you sense the Holy Spirit is saying to you and to the group.

Pray for one another.

Close in prayer.

Almighty and eternal God, so draw our hearts to you, so guide our minds, so fill our imaginations, so control our wills, that we may be wholly yours, utterly dedicated unto you; and then use us, we pray you, as you will, and always to your glory and the welfare of your people; through our Lord and Savior Jesus Christ. Amen.

Helpful Prayers

Rosh Chodesh Prayers: Sanctifying the Month
To be said at the first day of the new moon.
(The date of the new Jewish month can be found online.)

May it be your will Lord, God of our fathers,
that you begin for us this month for good, and for blessing.
May you give us long life, a life of peace, a life of goodness,
a life of blessing, a life of sustenance, a life of physical health, a life in
which there is no shame or humiliation, a life of wealth and honor,
a life in which we love your Word, and fear God, a life in which the
Lord fulfills the requests of our hearts for good. Amen.

We bless the moon in the name of our Lord Jesus Christ. We bless
the earth, the air, the water, and the fire. We thank you that the earth
is the Lord's and the whole earth is full of the glory of God. The sun
shall not smite us by day nor the moon by night. No created thing can
be used against God's people or His Kingdom in this month. We take
authority over all curses, hexes, spells, hoodoo, voodoo, sex magick,
soulish prayers, false words of prophecy, gossip, and Christian prayers
not of the Lord. We bless those who curse us, and commend you to
almighty God.

Psalms 113-118 are recited without pause.

A Prayer for Renewal

O Holy Spirit, come like a mighty rushing wind and
Awaken us out of our complacency, our apathy, and our indifference.
Disturb us,
For we are too content to let people go on
not knowing you.
Penetrate the closed gates of our hearts
and make us live again.
O Holy Spirit,
create among us a mighty Christian revolution
And cast the fear of the unknown out of our lives.[91]

The Belonging House Prayer

O Author of Beauty,
who first revealed yourself as Creator,
and filled Bezalel with the Holy Spirit.
Raise up an Army of Artists
who will build Jesus a Throne in the earth,
and make a way for the Coming of the Lord.
Fill us, renew us, and make us bearers of your glory.
May your Kingdom be established,
and your throne be extended
by the good work of our hands,
and the expressions of our creativity.
Through Jesus Christ, the Icon of the Invisible God, Amen.

The Prayer of Self-Dedication

Almighty and eternal God,
so draw our hearts to you,
so guide our minds,
so fill our imaginations,
so control our wills,
that we may be wholly yours,
utterly dedicated unto you;
and then use us, we pray you, as you will,
and always to your glory and the welfare of your people;
through our Lord and Savior Jesus Christ. Amen.

The Presence Prayer

Jesus,
I believe that You are in me,
and I am in You.
If I am in You, then I am in my Father,
and my Father is in Me,
Just as You are in the Father.
Thank you that I abide in You,
and Your word abides in me.
Because of this I can ask anything in Your Name,
I can do greater things than You did,
I can love others as You have loved me,
and by this, Your Father is glorified.

Anima Christi

Soul of Christ, sanctify me.
Body of Christ, save me.
Blood of Christ, inebriate me.
Water from Christ's side, wash me.
Passion of Christ, strengthen me.
O good Jesus, hear me.
Within your wounds hide me.
Suffer me not to be separated from you.
From the malicious enemy, defend me.
In the hour of my death, call me,
And bid me come unto you;
That I may praise you with your saints
and with your angels forever and ever,
Amen.

Prayer of Release from Cynicism

Dear Heavenly Father:
You tell us in the book of Proverbs that "hope deferred makes the heart sick." I have had my hopes deferred through disappointments with leaders, relationships, and institutions. Rather than accepting disappointments and offenses, and forgiving those who have not met my expectations; I have grown hard and calloused. I have become cynical.

I confess to you, almighty God, and to my brothers and sisters, that I have embraced the sin of cynicism and looked at it as even a nobler way of life than those who have "sold out." I have hid behind the mask of being "prophetic" or "discerning." I have allowed cynicism to manifest and hide the deadly sin of pride. Because of this, my prayers have been hindered. My pride has prevented my desires from being fulfilled and becoming a tree of life.

I choose to renounce cynicism and the root of pride. I humble myself before you and choose to embrace people, relationships, and opportunities, even if it means I may get disappointed or hurt. I choose to put my hope and trust in you, Lord, not in any human relationship or institution to fulfill my hopes and dreams. It is only in embracing this cross that I can experience the resurrection life of Jesus.

I forgive and release those who made promises that were not kept. I forgive those who thought they could meet my needs, but were unable as human creatures. I forgive the schools, churches, employers or governments, and any other area of human society that did not live up to my expectations. I now let go of any belief that they can meet my needs. I surrender to you, Father, and allow you the space to work.

I forgive myself for the sinful reaction to the disappointments of life. I ask you, Holy Spirit, to heal the hurt places, and remove the hardness of my own heart toward others.

I choose to become like a child, not purposely ignorant, but trusting in your grace and mercy; knowing that hope in you does not disappoint.

I make this prayer in the name of Jesus, who was despised and rejected by those he came to seek and save. Amen.

Works Cited

Baker Publishing Group. "The Great Emergence by Phyllis Tickle." YouTube Video, 2:45. October 8, 2008. https://youtu.be/YRtQM-5lO0aw?si=TrBJF5F_7EG7NyUg.

Bonhoeffer, Dietrich and Gerhard Leibholz. *The Cost of Discipleship*. Translated by Reginald H. Fuller. London: SCM Press, 1948.

Buckley, Michael and Tony Castle. *The Catholic Prayer Book*. London: Darton Longman & Todd, 1999.

Church of England and Society of St Francis. *Celebrating Common Prayer: A Version of the Daily Office SSF*. London: Mowbray, 1992.

Durant, Will. *The Story of Philosophy: The Lives and Opinions of the Greater Philosophers*. 2nd ed. New York: Simon & Schuster, 1926.

Global Awakening. "How To Overcome Trauma | Dr. Mike Hutchings | Unbroken Conference." YouTube Video, 1:19:55. May 15, 2023. https://youtu.be/SRAiziP5HpM?si=cOsnm8o6Uha0JTLf.

UnHerd, "Paul Kingsnorth: What is there left to conserve?" YouTube Video, 24:14. May 21, 2023. https://youtu.be/EObWLbJqG-kI?si=5ItwIbPbrXH2Izi-.

McNutt, Paula M. *The Forging of Israel: Iron Technology, Symbolism, and Tradition in Ancient Society*. London: A&C Black, 1990.

Otto, Christ John. *Bezalel: Redeeming a Renegade Creation*. Boston: Belonging House, 2015.

Ruthven, Jon Mark. *What's Wrong with Protestant Theology? Tradition Vs. Biblical Emphasis*. Tulsa, OK: Word & Spirit Press, 2013.

Tapscott, Betty. *Set Free Through Inner Healing*. Houston, TX: Hunter Ministries Publishing Company, 1978.

Tickle, Phyllis. *The Great Emergence: How Christianity Is Changing and Why*. Grand Rapids, MI: Baker Books, 2008.

Tuffs, Allan C., Paul Palnik and North American Federation of Temple Brotherhoods. *And You Shall Teach Them to Your Sons: Biblical Tales for Fathers and Sons*. New York: UAHC Press, 1997.

Whistler, James Abbott McNeill. *The Gentle Art of Making Enemies*. New York: Frederick Stokes & Brother, 1908. https://www.gutenberg.org/ebooks/24650

Whyte, David. "Loaves and Fishes." In *The House of Belonging*. Langley, WA: Many Rivers Press, 1997.

Endnotes

1   UnHerd, "Paul Kingsnorth: What is there left to conserve?" YouTube Video, 24:14, May 21, 2023, https://youtu.be/EObWLbJqGkI?si=5ItwIbPbrXH2Izi-.
2   I Chronicles 12:32.
3   Dietrich Bonhoeffer and Gerhard Leibholz, *The Cost of Discipleship*, trans. Reginald H Fuller (London: SCM Press, 1948), 87.
4   The Ten Commandments are the first ten of the 613 commandments given by God to the Jewish people. They form the foundation of Jewish ethics, behavior, and responsibility. These commandments are mentioned in order twice in the Torah - once each in the book of Exodus and the book of Deuteronomy.

1) I am the Lord thy god, who brought thee out of the land of Egypt, out of the house of bondage.
2) Thou shalt have no other gods before Me.
3) Thou shalt not take the name of the Lord thy God in vain.
4) Remember the Sabbath day to keep it holy.
5) Honor thy father and thy mother.
6) Thou shalt not murder.
7) Thou shalt not commit adultery.
8) Thou shalt not steal.
9) Thou shalt not bear false witness against thy neighbor.
10) Thou shalt not covet anything that belongs to thy neighbor.

https://www.jewishvirtuallibrary.org/the-ten-commandments.

5   Most of these points are covered in my book *Bezalel: Redeeming a Renegade Creation*. Christ John Otto, Bezalel: Redeeming a Renegade Creation (Boston: Belonging House, 2015).
6   Jon Mark Ruthven, What's Wrong with Protestant Theology? Tradition Vs. Biblical Emphasis (Tulsa, OK: Word & Spirit Press, 2013), 26.
7   I Corinthians 14:33.
8   This phrase, "Context is everything," was the first sentence said by Dr. Bob Lyon in my first week at Asbury Theological Seminary in 1993.
9   Zechariah 1:14-16.
10 Deuteronomy 28:1-14.
11 Revelation 21:23-27.
12 III John 2.
13 Zechariah 1:18-19, 21.
14 II Chronicles 2:13-14.
15 James Abbott McNeill Whistler, *The Gentle Art of Making Enemies* (New York: Frederick Stokes & Brother, 1908), https://www.gutenberg.org/ebooks/24650.
16 David Whyte, "Loaves and Fishes," in *The House of Belonging* (Langley, WA: Many Rivers Press, 1997).
17 II Corinthians 10:4-5.
18 Isaiah 44:9-19, NLT.

19 Paula M. McNutt, *The Forging of Israel: Iron Technology, Symbolism, and Tradition in Ancient Society* (London: A&C Black, 1990), 228.
20 "Hilma af Klimt & Piet Mondrian: Forms of Life," Tate Modern, accessed December 15, 2023, https://www.tate.org.uk/whats-on/tate-modern/hilma-af-klint-piet-mondrian.
21 Luke 4:8.
22 Joshua 24:15.
23 I Chronicles 25:1.
24 I Peter 2:5.
25 I Peter 2:9.
26 Isaiah 66:21-23.
27 Revelation 7:15-17.
28 Psalm 2:1-3, NLT.
29 Psalm 2:4-5, NLT.
30 Isaiah 61:3-4, NLT.
31 Zechariah 2:4-5.
32 Revelation 21:22-26.
33 I Corinthians 3:16, 6:19.
34 Baker Publishing Group, "The Great Emergence by Phyllis Tickle," YouTube Video, 2:45, October 8, 2008, https://youtu.be/YRtQM5lO0aw?si=TrBJF5F_7EG7NyUg.
35 Judges 21:25.
36 Romans 8:1-2.
37 I Samuel 2:35.
38 Hebrews 6:5.
39 I Samuel 7:3-4.
40 Joshua 24:14-24.
41 Matthew 7:12.
42 ISamuel 13:13-14.
43 John 4:23.
44 I Samuel 15:22-23.
45 Isaiah 6:5.
46 I Samuel 15:23.
47 I Samuel 13:14.
48 Allan C Tuffs, Paul Palnik and North American Federation of Temple Brotherhoods, *And You Shall Teach Them to Your Sons: Biblical Tales for Fathers and Sons* (New York: UAHC Press, 1997), 2.
49 I Samuel 17:36.
50 Will Durant, *The Story of Philosophy: The Lives and Opinions of the Greater Philosophers* (New York: Simon & Schuster, 1926), 87.
51 Psalm 27:10.
52 Psalm 116:16.
53 Global Awakening, "How To Overcome Trauma | Dr. Mike Hutchings | Unbroken Conference," YouTube Video, 1:19:55, May 15, 2023, https://youtu.be/SRAiziP5HpM?si=cOsnmSo6Uha-0JTLf.
54 Dr. Mike Hutchings, "8-Step Healing Prayer Model," Global Awakening, https://globalawakening.com/free-post-traumatic-stress-disorder-card/.

55   Adapted from a prayer by Francis MacNutt, Christian Healing Ministries.
56   Betty Tapscott, Set Free Through Inner Healing (Houston: Hunter Ministries Publishing Company, 1978).
57   Romans 6:12-14, The Jerusalem Bible.
58   Romans 12:1.
59   Philippians 2:5-11.
60   Colossians 1:27.
61   Ecclesiasticus 2:1-6.
62   I Chronicles 15:16-18.
63   I Chronicles 15:25-28.
64   Phyllis Tickle, *The Great Emergence: How Christianity Is Changing and Why* (Grand Rapids, MI: Baker Books, 2008), 10-11.
65   Genesis 49:10.
66   Psalm 132:1-5.
67   I Chronicles 17:4-14.
68   Psalm 132:11-12.
69   Isaiah 66:1-2.
70   Isaiah 66:12-1
71   Isaiah 66:18-23.
72   Matthew 7:15-20, Luke 6:43-45.
73   Wisdom of Solomon 13:3.
74   Mark 1:15.
75   Galatians 5:1.
76   John 14:9.
77   The daily gospel reading can be found online at universalis.com, or downloaded at almanac.oremus.org.
78   Matthew 18:20.
79   Revelation 18:21-24, NLT.
80   Matthew 10:34-36.
81   Matthew 10:16.
82   Revelation 19:1-7.
83   Daniel 7:13b-14.
84   Acts 1:6-11.
85   Zechariah 12:8.
86   Don Moen, "Jesus, We Enthrone You," track 9 on Praise with Don Moen, Hosanna! Music, 1995, compact disc.
87   Leviticus 27:9.
88   "Merry" Cardinal Del Val, 1926.
89   Adapted from "The Indian Prayer Before Sleep" in *Celebrating Common Prayer*. Church of England and Society of St Francis, *Celebrating Common Prayer: A Version of the Daily Office SSF* (London: Mowbray, 1992), 268. Used by permission.
90   Translation of an Orthodox hymn used at Malling Abbey, West Malling, Kent.
91   Adapted from a prayer by Michael Hollings and Etta Gullick in *The Catholic Prayer Book*. Michael Buckley and Tony Castle, *The Catholic Prayer Book* (London: Darton Longman & Todd, 1999), 47.

CHRIST JOHN OTTO
earned a B.S. in Christian Education
and Bible from Houghton College
and an M.Div.
from Asbury Theological Seminary.

He is the founder of Belonging House, an international fellowship of artists and creative people. He is the author of many books including the seminal work *Bezalel: Redeeming a Renegade Creation,* the first in-depth study of Bezalel in English.

Every Friday he sends an encouraging email to artists and creative people. You can find him at belonging.house, or at christjohnotto.substack.com

www.ingramcontent.com/pod-product-compliance
Lightning Source LLC
LaVergne TN
LVHW070525070526
838199LV00073B/6704